THE NEW SPIRIT OF TRUTH

THE NEW SPIRIT OF TRUTH

*Its Activity Today as Advocate
and Vehicle of the Holy Spirit*

RICK SPAULDING

WRIGHTWOOD PRESS

ANN ARBOR

Wrightwood Press
www.wrightwoodpress.org

Edited by Maurice York.
Book design and cover art by Maurice York.

NON-PROFITS, LIBRARIES, EDUCATIONAL INSTITUTIONS,
WORKSHOP SPONSORS, STUDY GROUPS, ETC.
Special discounts and bulk purchases are available.
Please email sales@wrightwoodpress.org for more information.

April 2023
ISBN 978-0-9801190-9-1

To Alice —
My wife and heart of our family,
prophetess of my writing project begun thirty years ago
and concluding with this twelfth book, as she foresaw;
director of an early intervention program
at Esperanza School for 18 years; and a pioneer in the
treatment of infant developmental problems.

We but mirror the world.
All the tendencies present in the outer world are to be found in the world of our body.
If we could change ourselves, the tendencies in the world would also change.
As a man changes his own nature, so does the attitude of the world change towards him.
This is the divine mystery supreme.
A wonderful thing it is and the source of our happiness.
We need not wait to see what others do.

—*Mahatma Gandhi*

CONTENTS

CHAPTER I:
SIDDHARTHA GAUTAMA

SIDDHARTHA GAUTAMA WAS BORN ABOUT 563 B.C. in northeast India to Suddhodana, the ruler of the Gautama warrior clan. Siddhartha had been preparing for his task for thousands of years, but this birth was his first actual incarnation. Until this time, he had only left the heavenly world to enter into the soul of one of his followers when the pupil had reached about the age of thirty. A great change occurred in the personality of the pupil when Siddhartha overshadowed or, more accurately, over-lighted his ego and pursued his task on the earthly plane. Many events in Greek mythology portray a similar occurrence when a Greek god or goddess entered a hero's soul and helped him or her to accomplish a mighty deed. Siddhartha had worked with many different pupils in this fashion, but no one knew which pupil he would choose until the great transformation in the pupil's personality became manifest. Buddhism refers to these incorporations as the preparations of a human bodhisattva. Only after this bodhisattva was fully ready to achieve his mighty task did he fully enter a human life and experience the difficulties bound up with childhood, adolescence, and young adulthood.

At the age of twenty-nine, Siddhartha left his home to seek "the supreme peace of Nirvana." He received instruction from two different religious teachers before finally undertaking extreme ascetic practices for six years. When he returned to a natural regimen and sat quietly in concentrated meditation, he attained enlightenment. As the Enlightened One, Gautama Buddha gave his first discourse at Benares around 528 B.C. In his exposition of his basic doctrine, he told of avoiding extremes and following the middle path to gain the enlightenment which consists of the realization of the Four Noble Truths. The Buddha felt compassion for his fellow human beings and sought to share his wisdom with them. He gathered many followers, including his pupils from former lives and formed a community—the Sangha. This order of monks became one of the three jewels of Buddhism along with the Buddha and the Doctrine.

Upon his transfiguration and death around 483 B.C., Gautama Buddha became an Ascended Master. In a single human lifetime, he had left the cycle of reincarnations and joined the hierarchy of angels. He was the sixth human being to have attained Buddhahood, the great ideal of earth's evolution. Gautama's achievement signaled that the earth had reached the midpoint in its spiritual development. Six other human bodhisattvas will also have to become Buddhas for the spiritual development of mankind to be complete. Buddhism refers to the seventh human bodhisattva as the Maitreya bodhisattva. He has already begun his preparations for the one full incarnation that he will undergo in the middle of the fifth millennium. He has begun to over-light various ones of his pupils at about the age of thirty and thereby prepare new spiritual talents and gifts so that he may incorporate them into the spiritual members of his inner being during his one full incarnation.

Five remaining human bodhisattvas, following the Maitreya bodhisattva, will have to carry out their missions before mankind can complete the human stage of its development and attain to freedom and love. These five bodhisattvas are different in one fundamental regard from those who have gone before them. They are presently undergoing full incarnations, while the six Ascended Masters and the future Maitreya Buddha will have fully incarnated only a single time each. These seven Buddhas of only a single incarnation can be called Eastern Masters, while the five human bodhisattvas can be called the Western Masters. To imitate Christ's service and sacrifice for the lowest and most oppressed people, the Western Masters try to help, heal, and educate as many people as possible. When they incarnate, they devote themselves to awakening as many human beings as possible so that the greatest number of people will be able to join the Ascended Masters in the heavenly world.

Certain signs accompany the birth of a human bodhisattva. Buddhism tells of an event that occurred to Queen Maya, Siddhartha's mother—how a white elephant overshadowed her and announced that Maya would give birth to a divine man: "And he will attune all beings to love and friendship and will unite them in a bond of religious fervor."[1] The wise men of India also knew of these signs. One of the Brahman (the highest caste of Hindu priests), Asiata, said of Siddhartha while he was just a baby: "This child is the one who will become a Buddha, the savior, the leader of immortality, freedom, and the light."[2]

Buddhist tradition suggests that a certain event occurs to a human bodhisattva around the age of twelve. Siddhartha went missing. When he was found later by his parents, he was sitting under a tree, surrounded by the poets and sages of the time, and conversing with them. Tradition also holds that the Tempter (Mara) came to the Buddha and promised him all the kingdoms of the earth. The Buddha responded: "I know well that I am destined to have a kingdom, but I do not desire an earthly one; I will achieve Enlightenment and make all the world rejoice."[3]

The key event in a Buddha's life is not outwardly visible. It is called Enlightenment and is said to occur under the Bodhi tree. Its result, however, is made known to others by the Enlightened One. When Gautama Buddha spoke at Benares, he revealed to all mankind the Four Noble Truths, the second jewel of Buddhism. This decisive event in a Buddha's life—Enlightenment—can be compared to the role the bodhisattva had played in the lives of his pupils. Whereas previously the human bodhisattva overshadowed his students, now the bodhisattva himself would be over-lighted by a Spirit of Truth—a divine bodhisattva. This powerful experience brings the path to the spirit world closer to mankind. It culminates in bringing new faculties into the soul of man, ennobling man's spiritual stature.

A final sign of the presence of a Buddha appears in the manner of his death. On a journey at the age of eighty, Siddhartha Gautama became ill. When the wagon in which he was riding stopped at a river, he lay down on a rug that his disciple, Ananda, had spread for him. Siddhartha's body began to shine from within. It then transformed into a body of light, a transfiguration that signified the end of his journey in the cycle of reincarnations and the beginning of his ego's union with the universe.

To grasp the divine bodhisattva properly requires understanding that the Spirits of Truth have been the leaders of mankind since the time of the outpouring of the human egos by the Elohim. Even before the time of Adam and Eve, when the earth itself was in a purely spiritual form, the Spirits of Truth guided human beings. These primeval teachers, however, had to withdraw from the earthly realm during the middle of the period which occultism designates as the Lemurian epoch, and which religious texts call the fall from paradise. Had they remained in the presence of human beings, the development of human freedom and of love as a gift freely given to another could never have occurred. The presence of a divine bodhisattva is simply too overwhelming. In 1924 in his lectures on *Karmic Relationships*, Rudolf Steiner explained that the primeval teachers withdrew to the moon sphere, to what religious traditions call purgatory or *kama loca*. There they greet newly departed human souls and lead them on a retrospective of their past life. They do not show them what actions, thoughts, and feelings the human ego had, but rather how such actions, thoughts, and feelings affected other human beings. The Spirits of Truth reveal the truth of our deeds and ideals and provide us with a mighty impulse to make up for our sins in the next life.

Divine bodhisattvas do not enter the earthly realm, with one exception only—the single instance when a Spirit of Truth enlightens the soul of a human bodhisattva. While Enlightenment remains hidden from the rest of the world, the Enlightened One can give report of it and inspire others with its truth. Just as there are twelve human bodhisattvas, so are there twelve Spirits of Truth. The six Ascended Masters each worked with a single Spirit of Truth. The deeds of the Eastern Masters have enabled their corresponding divine bodhisattvas to complete their tasks and hold on to everything they have accomplished as the foundation on which the future development of mankind can proceed. The idea that, altogether, twelve Spirits of Truth stand behind the advances humanity has made in the sphere of freedom and the creation of the cosmos of love is the reason that history speaks of the twelve tribes of Israel and the twelve disciples of Christ, and why science tells of the twelve months of the year and the twelve signs of the zodiac.

Just as a human bodhisattva can over-light one of his pupils and cause a change in the pupil's personality, so can a divine bodhisattva over-light his Master of Wisdom and bring about Enlightenment. The first jewel of Buddhism is simply the knowledge that Gautama became a Buddha—that Buddhahood is the goal for all mankind. When the Buddha spoke at Benares following his Enlightenment, the second jewel appeared in the world. The Four Noble Truths belong to the Spirits of Truth, as the name suggests. The fourth truth even allows the attentive listener to take up the path to the actual destination of earth's evolution. The eightfold path, as it is called in Buddhism, is known to other religions as well; in America, Benjamin Franklin used it in forming his own meditative path. Attaining the ideal of Buddhahood requires each human being to investigate his or her own soul and take up the task of daily meditation to allow the Spirits of Truth an opportunity to prepare the soul for reaching higher states of consciousness. Virtues can be formed, and new talents developed, not all at once, but step-by-step.

While most Westerners are not familiar with the soul organs that the people of the East call lotus flowers or chakras, they have taken an interest in meditation and self-development. In meeting the eightfold path, these would-be meditants have found a proper means for preparing the soul for a conscious entrance into the astral world and transforming dreams into genuine imaginations. The meditative exercises are safe and develop the petals of the throat chakram into the eight virtues—right opinion, right resolve, right word, right action, right standpoint, right ideal, right memory, and right self-examination. The truth of meditation gradually dawns on the sincere pupil—that meditation is not a selfish desire, but a preparation to bring good into the world, and that virtue is its own reward. Millions upon millions of people have taken up this path and found the gift of the Spirit of Truth meant to purify the human soul without having to join a secret society or take the risk of compromising their freedom. Rudolf Steiner even suggested that the first truly free action for most human beings is the decision to take up meditation. Buddha is one of the foremost examples of the meditant.

Many people know Buddha as the Lord of Compassion. His fundamental belief in the sacredness of all life is bound up with the feeling life and the power of love. Many modern people have experienced empathy by developing a sense for the feeling life in other people as well as in animals. The proliferation of pets through all cultures and societies would be otherwise hard to explain. Unfortunately, some people of the present time lack this faculty of the feeling life—this gift of the Lord Buddha. This lack is not a good thing, and exercises should be undertaken to develop it. Gautama Buddha also developed a corresponding virtue of the thought life and life of volition. The faculties of logical thinking and of the conscience as they later appeared in fourth century Athens suggests their source in fifth century India.

The home of the human bodhisattvas is called Nirvana, a word difficult to translate into Western languages. Rudolf Steiner suggested that it be translated as "the world of Providence" and that the twelve human bodhisattvas be called the Masters of Wisdom and the Harmony of Feelings. Western esoteric groups often refer to the home of the Masters as the White Lodge. From the descriptions given thus far of the activities of Masters like Gautama Buddha and the

Maitreya bodhisattva, the idea of calling Nirvana by the name of Providence seems suitable, since the efforts of the masters to bring future attributes into man's inner being depend upon living into the future.

The names of the gods can also be a source of confusion. In ancient times people were familiar with the names that a god took in one or another language. This idea is obvious in the case of the Greeks and Romans, even to the extent that Apollo had the same appellation in both languages. What also needs to be understood is that the Egyptians called him Osiris and the Hindus named him Krishna. Another example could be drawn from the days of the week. In English the names of the days are taken from Norse gods, but the Romance languages suggest that Tiu, Woden, Thor, and Freya refer to Mars, Mercury, Jupiter, and Venus. Even more important is an understanding of the hierarchy of angels—the nine classes of angels and the threefold nature of the godhead. Although the full hierarchy was known and studied in medieval Scholasticism, much of it stretched beyond the capacity of human understanding, and the Trinity itself was wrapped in mystery. The first three classes of angels, however, can be comprehended. Angels serve as guardians of individual human egos, while archangels work with groups of people and are called folk souls when they guide nations. The third class of angels is called the archai by Christian theology.

These time spirits work with various folk souls during the period of their rulership, for example, the Reformation during the sixteenth century in Europe. Altogether the first three classes of the angels constitute the third hierarchy, the next three classes form the second hierarchy, and final three classes make up the first hierarchy—the Seraphim, Cherubim, and Thrones who are closest to the Godhead.

Mahatma Gandhi experienced much difficulty in his life because of his honorific. He considered it to be a curse because the term "Mahatma" implied that he was an Ascended Master or the Maitreya bodhisattva. He wrote his autobiography in part, to show his imperfections and sins. He called it "An Autobiography: The Story of My Experiments with Truth." Gandhi clarified in his "Farewell"—the final chapter of his book—that being able to embody truth in his mind, his speech, and his actions was ever his goal. The one hundred and sixty- seven chapters of his book give, as it were, 167 instances of his attempts to achieve the purity of heart that the Spirit of Truth demands. Gandhi believed that God could enter the earthly realm, even if imperfectly, when Truth is realized as Ahimsa (non-violence) through Satyagraha (a movement based entirely upon Truth). "To see the universal and all-pervading Spirit of Truth face to face one must be able to love the meanest of creation as oneself."[4]

An avatar, in the Hindu view, is the incarnation of a god. The incarnation of Vishnu—one of the three chief deities in Hinduism—in Krishna is usually given to illustrate this idea. The importance of the *Bhagavad-Gita* rests on the role that Krishna plays as the avatar of Vishnu. In similar fashion Gautama Buddha can be viewed as the avatar of the Spirit of Truth. Rudolf Steiner took up this viewpoint and deepened it by characterizing a Spirit of Truth as a composite being. He suggested that three different members of the third Hierarchy—an angel, an archangel, and an archai—joined together to become an individual being. The incredible power of a Spirit of Truth—as shown in purgatory, or the moon sphere—derives from its simultaneous activation of Imagination, Inspiration, and Intuition in those human beings in its vicinity so that clairvoyance, clairaudience, and spiritual communion arise in their souls. In a passage of the Gospel of St. John, Christ told his disciples that they must not despair over his coming crucifixion, for only by his passing through the trial of death would He be able to ask the Father to send a new Spirit of Truth to them. This Spirit of Truth, He told them, would be able to abide with them and be the Comforter. The Christian view of the new Spirit of Truth even leads to the idea that it will serve as an avatar of the Holy Spirit—that the angel, archangel, and archai that the Father chooses will show such respect for freedom that these

14

members of the third hierarchy can become a vessel by which the third member of the Trinity can enter the earthly realm. The baptism by fire and the Holy Spirit is the realization of what Mahatma Gandhi worked to achieve with the Satyagraha Ashram.

NOTES FOR CHAPTER 1

[1] Rudolf Steiner, *Christianity as a Mystical Fact*, p.63.

[2] Ibid., p.64.

[3] Ibid., p. 65.

[4] Mahatma Gandhi, An Autobiography: The Story of My Experiments with Truth, p. 504.

CHAPTER 2:
ANCIENT GREECE

ISTORIANS GENERALLY VIEW HOMER AS THE
beginning of Western civilization. His epic, *The
Iliad*, opens with the words: "O Muse, speak through
me the wrath of Achilles." In addition, Homer offered
the Greeks *The Odyssey*. He gave the Greek people
heroes to emulate and helped make ancient Greece the
birthplace of democracy and freedom. What historians
often omit is the fact that Homer did not write a book
and read it to his audience, much less sell it and live off
the income. Rather, he recited his poem orally and
gave credit to the muse of epic poetry, Calliope. If
people wanted to hear it again, or for the first time,
Homer would have had to recite it from memory.
Other bards who had a similar power of memory could
listen to Homer and repeat the epic poem flawlessly.
Greece stood at the portal—the entranceway—to the
activity of the intellectual faculties in the inner being
of man.

The inauguration of the Olympic Games occurred
in 776 B.C. These games played a pivotal role in the

formation of the character of the Greek people. The various city-states of Greece ceased all wars they had been waging, and their people traveled to Mt. Olympus, the home of the Greek gods, to take part in the pentathlon and other sporting events. The pentathlon should not be confused with the modern Olympic Games or events like the World Series or the Super Bowl. Rather, it was a part of a religious festival and fell under the guidance of the mystery centers of Greece. Homer himself was an initiate of Zeus's oracle at Dodonna. His entire poem of about 24,000 lines was spoken in dactylic hexameter, a rhythm appropriate for walking. Whether the priests actually had the Greek participants take an active role in this unique situation that only occurred once every four years—an event that allowed all of Greece to hear of their national heroes and their mission to bring freedom into the world—has not been passed down through history to the modern day. By the time Homer's epic was written down several hundred years later, its perfection of rhythm and imagery was still intact. Over two millennia later, a Harvard professor of the classics even took on the Homeric task of memorizing *The Iliad* and spoke the entire epic from memory to his fellow Classics professors at their yearly gathering.

Calliope, the muse of epic poetry, served Apollo, who is generally credited with presiding over the birth of Greek culture. Epic poems other than those of

Homer are known to have existed during the early centuries of the Olympic Games, but they were not passed down to the other bards who could recall them when the time arose that they could be written down. When Melpomene—the muse of tragic poetry— became active in the fifth century B.C., she was even more directly connected with the Greek religion than was her sister muse. She inspired the Greek trage- dians—Aeschylus, Sophocles, and Euripides—whose trilogies were held in honor by all the citizens of Athens who were required to attend the amphitheater at the Temple of Dionysus. For a week in the spring of the year, five tragic poets were chosen to present their trilogies over five consecutive days. A winner was chosen to receive the prize, and the victor was cele- brated in a manner like that which the victor of the Olympic Games had once enjoyed.

When Socrates set out on his search to find a man wiser than himself, he discovered a note-worthy fact: the Greek dramatists lacked a conscious under- standing of their tragedies. They had been inspired by a Muse and could not explain in rational terms the deeper meaning of their plays. The high priest of the Temple of Dionysus was given the honor of sitting in the first seat of the first row of the middle aisle which divided the amphitheater in half. Socrates was seated across the aisle from him. Socrates was wise because he did not pretend to know the deeper meaning of what were called, in the Greek religion, the lesser mysteries. Melpomene inspired the Greek tragic poets with mythological pictures of the fire trial and the water trial in the lives of the great heroes, and these pictures were in turn presented to the people.

Aeschylus began taking part in the spring festival competition in 499 B.C. and directed his own plays. He won his first of twenty victories in 485 B.C. His trilogy of 458 B.C.—the only complete trilogy passed down through the corridor of time—also won the prize. The second play of *The Oresteia*, or "The Libation Bearers," tells of Orestes, the son of King Agamemnon, being ordered by Apollo to avenge the death of his father. Orestes carried out the divine mandate even though it meant taking the life of his own mother, Clytemnestra, who had murdered Agamemnon when he returned from Troy. Her evil deed could not go unpunished. In Aeschylus's play, when Orestes completed his task, the Furies arose from the underworld and sought retribution for his matricide. Orestes then fled to Athens to seek refuge, where Apollo arranged a trial to establish his guilt or innocence. In what historians view as the origin of the idea of a jury trial, Orestes was deemed innocent, and the avenging Furies transformed into the Eumenides, the goddesses of grace. When Euripides took up the same event in the third play of his trilogy, he did not bring the avenging Furies onto the stage. Rather, he had Orestes speak of how his conscience was attacking him and filling him with guilt. Seventy-five years after the transfiguration of Gautama Buddha, Euripides spoke of this new faculty of conscience, which would gradually become the common experience of all the citizens of Athens.

The priests of the Greek religion—in particular, the leaders of the Temple of Dionysius—brought the lesser mysteries and the truth of conscience to the Greek people through the spring festival. Much more important was the fall festival, where the greater mysteries were presented. While the spring festival was opened to all citizens, only certain Athenians were allowed to attend the fall mysteries—the mystae or initiates. They had to travel twenty or more miles to the town of Eleusis where in the temple of Demeter they experienced the truth embedded in the myth of Persephone—the secret of the reincarnation of the human soul. The same truth that Virgil's epic, *The Aeneid*, would reveal to the Romans four hundred years later was the basis for the performance of the sacred drama of Eleusis.[1]

The golden age of Athens is often called the Age of Pericles, after the famous leader who filled the city of Athens with the creations of master architects and sculptors such as Ictinus and Phidias. One of the seven wonders of the ancient world arose during the closing phase of the heyday of the great Greek dramatists. The statue of Athena, the namesake of the city, graced the

Parthenon. An even larger statue of her rose in the city's center and could be seen by sailors on the Aegean Sea. The Parthenon itself was a temple. In its underground chambers—in its inner sanctum—lay the sacred talisman that Odysseus had taken from Troy and that had eventually arrived in Athens, carefully guarded. The Palladium, named for the sister of Pallas Athena, had granted Troy protection so that the city could rule for a millennium. As it had done for Troy, so it would for Athens.

Apollo and the nine Muses—the inspiring angels of literature and the arts—stood behind the height of culture that the city of Athens attained in the fifth century B.C. The Romans also looked to Apollo as the wellspring from which arts and literature would grow and flourish. They even used the Greek word for his name, while all the other Roman gods (save two) had Latin names. In ancient Egypt, Apollo went by the name of Osiris. The people of ancient India knew him by the name of Krishna. India's greatest epic, *The Bhagavad-Gita* ("The Song of the Blessed One"), arose at the time of the glory of Greece, and it is still used today as the principal meditation in many a person's life.[2]

Another realm of culture, but not one associated with Apollo, also flourished in ancient Greece and especially in Athens. The sphere of philosophy, math, and science began to shine with the emergence of the pre-Socratic thinkers. Even more important was the contribution of Pythagoras. While his school did not attain great fame, it laid a sound basis for the teaching of mathematics, beginning with the memorization of the times tables and including the theorem named for him. Plato gave pre-eminence to mathematics as well. The doorway to the entrance of his school, The Academy, had a sign above it which read: "Let none but geometricians enter here." Teaching principles from arithmetic to spherical trigonometry, Plato prepared his students to understand the astronomical concept named after him—the Platonic year. His students learned how the twelve signs of the zodiac formed the world clock of the twelve Spirits of Truth, and how the vernal equinox could be used to tell time. The Platonic year of 25,920 earthly years is composed of twelve ages whose midpoints correspond to the twelve numbers on a watch or a clock. Plato used Ptolemaic astronomy to establish the beginning of the Greco-Roman age, which began in 747 B.C.—about the time of Homer. He also brought the mystery wisdom of Eleusis and of other mystery centers in Greece, Egypt, and Asia Minor to the light of day. In this regard, his *The Republic* is his most famous dialogue, but his four dialogues on the trial and death of his teacher, Socrates, demonstrate in a humanly objective way how "the unexamined life is not worth living."

Aristotle took the final step of uniting philosophy with logic. His study of nature enabled human beings to understand the surrounding world. His remarkable achievement was spread throughout the East by his even more famous pupil, Alexander the Great. On Alexander's journey through Asia Minor, Egypt, and the Middle East, he was able to found schools of philosophy and libraries such as the one at Alexandria. Often Alexander's generals did not have to fight battles, for he brought with him a casket bearing the golden *Iliad*. It helped clarify to the wise men of Egypt and elsewhere that Alexander wished to find homes for Greek culture, rather than make enemies through military conquests.

Through Alexander's expedition, Philosophia could continue her development and logical thinking could emerge in the East, and later, in the Muslim world. Steiner examines the full course of this angel's evolution in *The Riddles of Philosophy*. Steiner considered the faculty of logical thinking to be one of the great gifts of Gautama Buddha. With his attainment of Buddhahood, Gautama's angel no longer had the task of being his guardian. His angel became Philosophia and brought a genius for logic to other human souls who were open to it. Just as the lord of Compassion embodied empathy in his feeling life, so did his life of thought become filled with logic—an active thinking able to attain to the truth. The development of the conscience signaled the proper means to ennoble human volition. This inner voice allows human beings to act in freedom.

The hero Odysseus foreshadowed a further development of the intellect by the ancient Greek people. The goddess Athena placed the wily Odysseus under her personal protection during the Trojan War. In return, he brought the talisman of her sister to the city named for the goddess of wisdom, Athens. Raphael's painting, "The School of Athens," shows how the intellect advanced under the tutelage of Philosophia from the time of Plato and Aristotle down to that of the Italian masters. Concomitant with the appearance of the intellect was the gradual diminution of memory and the advent of books—such as those of Herodotus, the father of history—and their storage in vast libraries. The first true philosopher, Aristotle, developed logic and enabled human beings to attain the truth out of their own active thinking and in freedom. In the Western world, a lost of insight into karma and reincarnation was the unfortunate consequence of the shift of man's attention to the physical world surrounding him, accompanied by an ever more thorough investigation of it.

For centuries Michael served as the folk soul of the Hebrew people, but he began to withdraw prior to the time of the Babylonian captivity. His scene of activity shifted to Northern Europe and the Celtic tribes. The legends of King Arthur often point back to pre-Christian times when the king would gather his twelve knights of the Round Table and wait for an adventure to befall one or another of them on one of the four festival days of the year. With the coming of the seventh century B.C. and the beginning of a new sun regency, Michael shifted his sphere of activity to Greece and, in particular, to its mystery centers and oracles. The sun oracle in Greece in the fourth age of the post-Atlantean epoch was a kind of repetition of the fourth age of the epoch that preceded the Great Flood, which is called the Atlantean epoch. The fourth age was the time of the great evil, the fall of the Mars oracle as well as other oracles and mystery centers. Only the sun oracle of Michael remained free from corruption, and its role in the preservation of the mysteries became that much greater. This event of pre-history contains the unconscious reason that the ancient Greek people never built a temple to Ares (Mars) and never honored his name.

Due to their hatred for Mars, the Greeks honored the sun oracle, the temple at Delphi, all the more. While the common people, because of their devotion to mythology, viewed Apollo to be the god of truth and prophecy, the initiates, the mystae, knew that the actual archangel of the sun was Michael, who was the one who guided the city-states of Greece. Their kings and queens came to Mt. Parnassus to receive prophecies on all important occasions. Michael planted democracy first in Athens and nurtured its development in preparation for the day when he would release the cosmic intellect into the care of human beings.

Guarding the cosmic intelligence until mankind was sufficiently mature to use it in freedom required him to guide the city-states through the oracles of the Pythia. Most importantly, Michael was the guardian of Apollo, protecting him at all times from the same danger of youth and adolescence that required bodhisattvas to over-light their pupils when they had reached about the age of thirty.

Alexander the Great's success was only partly due to the activity of Apollo in Egypt and Philosophia in Persia. Alexander was victorious mainly due to Michael's activity as the planetary archangel of the sun. There are seven planetary archangels all together, each of whom serve, in rotation, as the leader for a period of 365 years. Michael took on his regency in 676 B.C., and his rulership lasted 365 years. Michael had ruled previously at the beginning of the Egyptian age as the Babylonian god, Marduk. At the time of Moses and the escape of Israel from the bonds of slavery, he was given his present name, "the face of the Elohim," or Michael. He became the Lord of Hosts who could not be opposed and was ever victorious. The sun regency of Michael in the Greek age came to an end in 311 B.C., after Alexander had completed his journey to ancient India.

The development of culture in ancient Greece is called in Freemasonry the pillar of beauty. It began with the founding epics of Homer. *The Iliad* pictured the emergence of human freedom in the Greek heroes as well as the spread of the decadence of patriarchy among the Trojans. *The Odyssey* showed the development of the intellectual soul against the spiritual background of Athena's inspirations. The city named after her, Athens, became the birthplace of democracy under the protective shield of Theseus. The tragedies of Aeschylus, Sophocles, and Euripides raised Greek culture to a higher level—its second stage—by bringing pictures of initiation into the lesser mysteries to the purview of the entire citizenry of Athens in the fifth century B.C. This Golden Age of Greece also saw the creation of the Parthenon and its statue of Athena. The architecture and sculpture of the Age of Pericles turned the city itself into an artistic masterpiece. The final stage of Greek culture was more hidden from Athenian citizens, save for those who were granted entrance into Plato's Academy or Aristotle's Lyceum. Plato unfolded to his pupils the wisdom in *The Dialogues*, and Aristotle the truth within his treatises during his long walks through the Lyceum. Alexander founded schools of philosophy throughout the East to preserve the works of Plato and Aristotle against the coming of the dark ages.

The closing event in the development of Greek culture occurred more than half a century after the journey of Alexander and brought the founding of Greek culture full circle, as it were. The epics of Homer told of the second generation of heroes—of

Achilles and Troy, of Odysseus and his voyage—while *The Argonautica*, the epic of Apollonius of Rhodes written around 250 B.C., tells of the first generation of heroes—of Hercules and the Argonauts, of Medea and the house of Colchis. Apollonius's poem describing the epic tale of Jason and the Golden Fleece completed the development of Greek culture by shedding the light of Calliope on its founding—the return of the Golden Fleece to the oracle of Apollo.

NOTES FOR CHAPTER 2

[1] Edouard Schure, *The Sacred Drama of Eleusis*.

[2] Mahatma Gandhi, *The Story of My Experiments with Truth* (morning meditation, dictionary of images, of people, and of events in daily life).

CHAPTER 3:
ANCIENT ROME

THE MISSION OF THE ANCIENT GREEKS WAS TO bring individual freedom and democracy into a vibrant, living culture, while that of the Romans was to establish the rule of law within a republican form of government. Unlike the Greeks, the Romans worshipped Mars and viewed him as the father of Romulus. The populace of Rome was composed of criminals and brigands. By establishing strict laws and rigorously enforcing them, the Roman Senate hoped to keep its citizens living with each other in peaceful community.

From the time of the formation of the Roman senate in 508 B.C., the combination of the worship of Mars, devotion to the art of warfare, respect for the law, and obedience to its tenets molded the Roman character. By the time of the Second Punic War three centuries later, the Romans were famous for their valor and sense of duty, much like the Spartans had been in ancient Greece. When Hannibal invaded Italy after crossing the Alps, he defeated the Roman army in several battles. Fabius the Delayer realized that the only hope for the Roman army was to avoid battle. The Roman general kept his troops in the high ground, the mountains, and shadowed Hannibal instead of engaging him. Though Hannibal roamed the countryside freely, he could not defeat the Roman legions. When he at last came to the city of Rome, he declined sending his soldiers inside its gates, even though young children, women, and the elderly were all who remained in its precincts. Hannibal's army stayed a safe distance away. Out-maneuvering and ambushing the Roman army was not the same as entering the lair of the god of war, Mars. The Romans finally sent an army across the Mediterranean Sea. As brilliant a general as Hannibal was, he met his match after his army was recalled to defend Carthage. Under the command of Scipio, the Roman legions defeated Hannibal, destroyed Carthage, and earned their general the title of Africanus.

Scipio then undertook the mission to bring the Palladium from its holy sanctuary in Athens, within the Parthenon, to Rome and its new home in the Temple of Vesta. This talisman had guarded Troy for a millennium and then protected Athens throughout the period of its golden age. It could only be handled by a man of spotless character. Scipio Africanus—the reincarnated Odysseus—was such a man, and he accomplished again for Rome what he had once done for Greece.

In the middle of the first century B.C., civil war broke out in Rome. Julius Caesar attempted to become the king of Rome but was foiled by the conspiracy of Brutus and Cassius. They, in turn, were defeated by Antony and Octavian. When the legions of the two remaining Roman generals fought each other to decide who would rule the Roman Empire, Octavian emerged victorious. Octavian encouraged the Senate to continue with its duties. He trained civil servants, installed Roman government officials in the various provinces of the empire, and instructed them to cooperate with the customs of the people in their region. He even allowed some provinces to have a degree of self-government. He built the Roman roads that brought the peoples of the empire together, protecting them with the Roman army so that trade could flourish.[1] In a word, Caesar Augustus ushered in the *Pax Romana* which lasted for over two hundred years.

Historians characterized the activity of the She-wolf of Rome during the time of the reign of Augustus until that of Marcus Aurelius by their use of the term, "the evil emperors." They also pointed to her activity by calling "bread and circuses" the main source of the corruption of the Roman sense of duty and valor. Even during the rulership of Augustus, her activity can be discerned. The idea that she might in fact oppose the coming of the Christ spirit into the earthly realm should not be hard to grasp. The Gospel of Matthew tells of the Roman governor of Galilee, Herod the Great, meeting with the three Magi and plotting with the Sanhedrin to kill the Messiah. History books identify Herod as born in Palestine of Arab parents, and as a Jew who was devoted to the religion of Abraham. He received his appointment to his provincial post through his friendship with Agrippa. He built fortresses and cities in Galilee and even rebuilt the Temple of Solomon during a tenure that stretched back to 37 B.C. Historians characterize Herod as cruel and superstitious. Even though he had ten wives, he was also said to be exceedingly jealous. Some historians have even connected the worsening of these flaws with the advent of "mental decay." Augustus received reports of Herod's disintegration but did not replace him before he died in 4 B.C., shortly after the "slaughter of the innocents" in Bethlehem.

The She-wolf's first attempt to employ an evil emperor to attain her goal of depriving human beings of freedom came in 37 A.D. Caligula became the third Roman emperor. The Roman people at first saw in him the promise of a good and fair emperor, but he suffered from an illness soon after being raised to the office of emperor; upon his recovery, he began to behave erratically, turn on his opponents, and indulge in great cruelty. He became known for his extravagance and waste—one of the most egregious being the construction of a two-mile-long pontoon bridge over the

Bay of Naples, upon being raised to office, in response to an opponent's remark that he had a better chance of riding a horse over the bay than becoming emperor of Rome. Early in his reign, he began making a pretense of divinity. While it had become common for leaders of Rome to be deified after death, Caligula broke all norms by demanding to be worshipped as a living deity. He extended his personal palace to the grand temple of Castor and Pollux, central to the city, wishing the temple to be the entrance to his own residence. Late in his reign, in response to religious unrest that broke out in Judea, he attempted to have a statue of himself erected in the Temple of Solomon, both desiring to be worshipped as a living god and believing that his presence could settle the political-religious controversy that had arisen.

Caligula was a nickname meaning "little boot" that Gaius Caesar Germanicus received from the Roman legionnaires who followed his father, their general. Unfortunately, Roman historians are not in agreement about his character. No less a historian that the great Tacitus wrote a history of Caligula's reign, but sadly and mysteriously it was lost somewhere in the corridor of time, one of his few histories not to survive. We may imagine the activity of the She-wolf was probably at work. She would be the only beneficiary of hiding the truth of Caligula's affection for his sister, Drusilla, and misleading historians into believing that he was handsome, well-educated, and intelligent. The events surrounding his death in 41 A.D. after ruling for three years and ten months, however, are not in dispute. Caligula had lost all his popularity and all the savings that Tiberius, the previous emperor, had amassed. He was murdered by a tribune of the Praetorian guard. The soldiers entrusted with the emperor's protection turned on him.

Thirteen years after Caligula's death in 54 A.D., Rome raised Nero to the office of emperor. His mother, Agrippina, had married Claudius I and after his death managed have her own son supplant Claudius's son by his first wife. She is credited with poisoning her husband so that she, the power behind her seventeen-year-old son, could become the effective ruler. She even had her name and bust placed on Roman coins. Nero's tutor, the philosopher Seneca, refused to cooperate with her schemes, and Nero retaliated against her and forced her into retirement in 56 A.D. and had her murdered three years later. When Rome went along with Nero's justification for her death, he concluded that he could do whatever he pleased. Leaving the government to Seneca's direction, he indulged in riotous nighttime parties, raced chariots, played the lyre, and acted on the stage. The Romans viewed his behavior as infamous breaches of decorum. By 62 A.D., Seneca retired. Nero then began to grow suspicious about possible rivals and had men removed from the Roman government whose lineage made them seem dangerous.

The Great Fire of Rome in 64 A.D. was blamed on Nero, probably unjustly. Romans thought that he wanted Rome to burn so that he could indulge in his aesthetic dreams for its reconstruction. The homelessness and starvation that resulted from the fire did lead Nero to perhaps the worst of his excesses. In an effort to deflect blame for the fire, Nero accused Christians of setting the fire and causing many other problems besetting Rome. The persecutions of Christians included putting them in the arena and having them eaten by lions. The influence of the She-wolf on Nero is likely since the Romans knew little about Christians or Jews. Nero is blamed for the murders of Peter and Paul in 64 A.D. He also promoted the idea of "bread and circuses" and accelerated the undermining of the Roman virtues of duty and loyalty. Finally, in 68 A.D., with everyone turned against him, Nero slit his own throat.

While the Roman Empire with its good and evil emperors took the leading role on the stage of world history, in obscurity a new religion was founded. The record of its founding is largely contained in the first four books of the New Testament of the Christian Bible. The gospels of Matthew, Mark, Luke, and John were not written down until many years after the crucifixion of Christ. The discussions in chapter two, "Ancient Greece," of how the Homeric epics came about may help explain how inspirations from the Gospel authors could have come down from the spiritual world even centuries after they occurred in the earthly realm. Insight into the meaning of the events described in the Gospels may also require knowledge of other religions. In the Matthew gospel, an angel of the Lord announces to Joseph that his wife would give birth to a child and that he should name him Jesus. This event corresponds to an angelic announcement to the parents, discussed previously as a sign of the birth of a human bodhisattva. When three wise men came from the East, they stopped in Jerusalem to meet with King Herod the Great about the coming birth of the King of Kings. Herod told the three kings that they should inform him when they found the child since he wished to honor him. The angel of the Lord, however, warned the three Magi not to return to Herod and then appeared to Joseph to tell him to flee into Egypt. Since the wise men avoided Herod, the king of Judea convened the Sanhedrin and asked them where the Messiah would be born. The scholars of the Torah told Herod that the Messiah would be born in Bethlehem, fulfilling the second sign of a bodhisattva's birth—the confirmation of the prophecy by wise men. Why Herod, a Jew, would want to kill the Messiah is not explained in the Matthew gospel. Some historians view the slaughter of the innocents in 4 B.C. to be a sign of Herod's diseased mind, suggesting that

Emperor Augustus knew of his madness and failed to replace him quickly enough. With Herod the Great's death shortly after ordering the atrocity, the angel of the Lord told Joseph to return to Bethlehem. Joseph was afraid of Herod's son, who had become the new King of Judea, as much as he had feared his father. Instead of going to Bethlehem, Joseph took his family to Nazareth to avoid the cruelty and dissipation of Archelaus Herod.

A second remarkable birth occurred in Bethlehem four years later. In the first year of the Common Era (1 A.D.), Caesar Augustus caused all the world to be taxed to put the Roman peace on a firm financial footing. Roman historians were as clear about its date as they were about the date of King Herod the Great's murderous rage and death. The first sign of a bodhisattva's birth—an angelic announcement to the parents—is included in the Gospel of St. Luke. The archangel Gabriel appeared to Mary and announced that she would bear a son through the activity of the Holy Spirit, and that she should name him Jesus. Gabriel also told her that her cousin, Elizabeth, was going to give birth to a child soon. Mary then travelled to see Elizabeth. When she arrived, the child in Elizabeth's womb began to kick. The Holy Spirit over-lighted Elizabeth (through the agency of a Spirit of Truth), and announced that Mary was most blessed among women, for she would become the mother of the Lord.

After spending about three months with her cousin, Mary returned to her home in Nazareth. She and Joseph then followed Caesar Augustus's command to return to their ancestral home to be taxed. Since Joseph was of the house and lineage of David, they travelled to the town of Bethlehem. Mary gave birth to a child on December 25, 1 A.D., while in the fields an angelic choir sang tidings of great joy to the shepherds watching their sheep. Before returning to their home in Nazareth, in accord with the Mosaic law, Mary and Joseph took their child to the temple in Jerusalem. The devout Simeon was over-lighted by the Holy Spirit, and he came into the temple and saw the child Jesus. He announced publicly that Jesus would become the salvation of mankind, fulfilling by his confirmation the second sign of a bodhisattva's birth. Anna, a prophetess, joined Simeon in giving thanks for the child.

A third remarkable birth, the one involving Elizabeth and Zachariah's child, also exhibited the signs of the birth of a bodhisattva. Gabriel, the moon archangel, announced to Zachariah that his wife would give birth to a child whose name should be called John, a child who would have the power of Elijah and who would be filled with the Holy Spirit. Since Elizabeth was barren and exceedingly old, Zachariah did not believe the archangel. Gabriel, expecting better of a priest in the Lord's temple, struck him dumb. After

Elizabeth gave birth to the child and wanted to name him John, some of their relatives objected. Zachariah settled the argument by writing on a tablet that John should be his name. Suddenly his tongue was loosed, and he began to praise God. The question of whether such signs—annunciation to a parent and, later, confirmation of a prophecy by a wise man—indeed mean that a bodhisattva is being born can be answered in the case of the child who became John the Baptist. When questions arose amongst His disciples about which prophet John the Baptist might have been, Christ told them that no one born of woman was greater than John (Matthew 11:11) and that John was the reincarnated Elijah (Matthew 11:14). That description of John defines him as a Master of Wisdom and a human bodhisattva.

The birth of the first Jesus child on Three King's day—January 6, 4 B.C.—hints at the identity of the bodhisattva who incarnated on that day. The three kings were called the Magi because they were followers of the Zoroastrian religion. They had travelled from the East to bring the gifts of gold, frankincense, and myrrh to the reborn Zoroaster—to Zarathustra. A deeper understanding of this truth should lead to the insight that the various religions of the world are not opposed to one another but form a unity. The founders and leaders of Buddhism (Gautama), Zoroastrianism (Zarathustra), Judaism (Elijah), and

Christianity brought the activity of the Spirits of Truth into the world. Gandhi sacrificed his life for this ideal in an effort to end the strife between Hinduism and Islam and to bring India into the modern age in a healthful way. The fact that religions tend to fall away from the high purposes that they were meant to serve does not mean that the lives of the human bodhisattvas were in vain. Rather, these pathways to the spirit must be brought into the sphere of freedom and become a blessing for all people.

Before discussing the identity of the Bodhisattva-like human being who stood behind the second Jesus child, it is important to clarify that the child whose birth is described in the Matthew gospel is not the same child as in Luke's gospel. They were born in two different years, (4 B.C. and 1 A.D.) and their parents lived in two different hometowns (Bethlehem and Nazareth). Each gospel also has a genealogy, and the two genealogies are completely different for many generations until the birth of the child that an angel had told the parents to name Jesus. While Christianity has for centuries preached "one Jesus," it is notable that the dates for Christ's birth are distinctly different for the two major branches of the Church, the Eastern and Western. The Orthodox churches celebrate Christmas on January 6th, while Catholic and Protestant churches celebrate it on December 25th. The ideal of the unity of religions is further elevated when the Spirit of Truth active in the human bodhisattvas and inspiring the authors of Holy Scripture can become illuminated and recognized.

It is easier to understand the identity of the second Jesus by closely examining the third sign that appears in the life of a human bodhisattva—having gone missing at the age of twelve and being found in discussions with wise men. The third sign is clearly given in the Luke gospel, but is absent in the Matthew gospel. The experience at the age of twelve is a kind of preparation for the transformation that will occur at age thirty. A bodhisattva at age thirty over-lights the student that he has chosen, or, if the bodhisattva is in his first full incarnation, a Spirit of Truth then over-lights him to bring his mission to fruition. The Luke Jesus experienced the third sign. He was over-lighted by a human bodhisattva, and thus his whole personality changed. The knowledge of a great bodhisattva began to shine in the wisdom that the Luke Jesus could now impart to others.

To fully grasp the Luke Jesus, the importance of his genealogy being traced back to Adam must be understood. The bodhisattva-like human being who was born in a manger according to the gospel of Luke experienced the over-lighting of an actual human bodhisattva (the Zarathustra ego) at the age of twelve. The Matthew Jesus was fifteen years old at the time of Passover in 12 A.D. The Matthew gospel mentions no events in the life of Jesus from the time of his return from Egypt in 4 B.C. until his Baptism by John in 30 A.D. The Baptism in the Luke gospel, as in the Mark gospel, is described as the coming down from the heavens of a Spirit in the form of a dove and the Son of God entering therein. Against the background of a Spirit of Truth entering a human bodhisattva as discussed previously in the picture of Gautama under the Bodhi tree, the entrance of the Christ spirit into a human body finds its precedent. The difference is that a human bodhisattva could prepare a body so that in thirty years a Spirit of Truth could enter and mediate the Holy Spirit's activity in the earthly realm—the baptism by fire and the Holy Spirit. For the Sun Spirit to mediate the Son principle of the Godhead to mankind, a special human body free from the influences of the fall of man in the garden of Eden had to be formed. Rudolf Steiner pointed to the creation of such a being when he called Apollo the sister-soul of Adam. Given into the care of Michael, the sun archangel, Apollo would later help inspire beauty to come into the world through arts and literature.

The requirement for a special human body free from the influence of the forces of evil helps explain the willingness of Herod the Great, a minion of the She-wolf, to commit such an atrocity as the slaughter of the innocents. This attempt having failed, the Luke Jesus was able to reach the age of twelve, when the new activity of the ego of Zarathustra would not conflict with the life and growth in the early years of his life, but rather foster the development of his mind and his spiritual faculties. But with the entrance of the Christ spirit at the turning point of time, the Zarathustra ego had to excarnate and only the avatar of Apollo could remain. The bodhisattva-like human being, Apollo—or Krishna, to use the Hindu terminology—had never fully incarnated before, yet experienced being over-lighted first by the Master Jesus at age twelve and then by the Christ at age thirty. A Master of Wisdom has much truth to teach, and the Spirit of Love said and did much in the following three years to bring the truth to life. Apollo's memories appear in the Holy Scriptures and in the glorious paintings of the Italian Masters.

The activity of two human bodhisattvas and a bodhisattva-like human being was needed to prepare the way for Christ, not only to have a Spirit of Truth enter into it and bring the Holy Spirit into the earthly realm, but to prepare a body for the Christ spirit to incarnate into—a body that would become a vessel for the second member of the Trinity, the Son, to accomplish the turning point of time. "The Spirit Light of the world stepped into the stream of earthly life."² What other human bodhisattvas do only once, both Elijah, as John the Baptist, and Zarathustra, as the Master Jesus, accomplished by experiencing birth, incarnating, and living through the vicissitudes of childhood and young adulthood. They came together on January 6, 30 A.D.

at the baptism in the Jordan River. The Master Jesus had shared the body of the second Jesus with the soul of Apollo since over-lighting him at the age of twelve. When the Sun Spirit in the form of a dove entered the body of Jesus, the human bodhisattva had fulfilled his task. The Master Jesus then excarnated. John the Baptist had likewise fulfilled his mission of preparing the way for the Messiah and was treacherously murdered not long afterwards.

These Masters of Wisdom began a process that would unite them with two other human bodhisattvas who had also been born and grew up to live an earthly life while Christ Jesus walked the earth. During that time, Christ was told of the death of Lazarus, whom he brought back to life as Lazarus/John. Christ also raised the young man of Nain from the dead. Up until the turning point of time, initiation had involved the activity of angels and archangels over-lighting the pupil of initiation. With the advent of Christ, a new path of self-development was being forged. The five "Western" bodhisattvas have not forsaken their tasks of becoming Buddhas, but they have learned of the importance of leading a full human life from Christ Jesus. The lessons they have taken in will form the subject of the movements that they will lead when they are born again in future ages.

The situation of the Jesus child born on December 25th of the first year of the Common Era was funda-

mentally different than that of the two Masters who sacrificed themselves to achieve the Baptism on the day of
Epiphany. It also differed from the impulses from Christ
that those Masters received that would become the missions of their future lives. The Apollo soul, the sister-soul
of Adam, was experiencing his first full incarnation. For
his first twelve years he was guided by his parents. For
the next eighteen years he was overshadowed by the
Zarathustra ego in a similar fashion to the way that
Zarathustra had entered into many of his pupils. After
the Baptism in the Jordan River, Jesus experienced what
Hinduism meant by saying that Krishna was an avatar, a
vessel for Vishnu. The difference was that in the Baptism an earthly incarnation was taking place and not the
over-lighting of a spiritual entity. Apollo was not sup-
pressed nor was he overshadowed by the Christ spirit.
Rather, he was observing and learning, for the goal of
Christ's earthly activity was to enable mankind to be free
so that people can act out of love.

One of Christ's disciples was a human bodhisattva. Lazarus, whom Christ raised from the dead,
became John, the disciple whom He loved. John's gospel, his letters, and his Revelations all play an
important role in elucidating Christ's plan for the
future of mankind, which He shared with His disciples. Christ wanted to tell them the truth about His
coming trial and crucifixion and to help them understand that His sacrifice was not a bad thing, that good

would come from it. In chapters 14 to 16 of the gospel of John, Christ Jesus told his disciples that He would build a place for them in heaven. If we would ask what this place might look like, then we would have to turn from John's gospel to his Revelations. In this book, John presented his vision of the New Jerusalem. It possessed twelve foundation stones, with twelve gates that opened out to pathways. John's vision of a completely formed New Jerusalem showed the realm of the heavenly world, which can also be called Providence, and which is also known in Buddhism by the Sanskrit name "Nirvana." Buddhists believe that it is only accessible to human bodhisattvas, Ascended Buddhas, and Spirits of Truth. The number of stones and gates John described in New Jerusalem envisions that the twelve Spirits of Truth will be active until the end of the cycles of the earth.

At the Passover supper before His crucifixion, Christ Jesus explained to his disciples that He was leaving the earthly world to go to heaven and prepare a place for them (John 14:2), He also said that He would come again to them so that they would be able to join Him in the heavenly kingdom that He was building for them. St. Paul's experience before the city of Damascus—the great vision he beheld there that drove him to his knees—can be viewed as an anticipation, or first instance, of what Christ was trying to explain about his Second Coming. Not an actual physical event—a second bodily incarnation of the Christ, or a "reincarnation"—but an actual imagination like the one that Paul saw can inspire human beings to take up a path of service toward their fellow brothers and sisters. Our work in the physical world can express the high ideals that we hold dear, and the joy that we take in realizing them in freedom expresses our love.

Christ Jesus offered His disciples a second reason for them not to be sad. He said that if He would undergo the trial awaiting Him, then He could ask the Father to send a new Spirit of Truth to mankind. In chapter one, the twelve Spirits of Truth were discussed as the spiritual leaders standing behind the twelve human bodhisattvas, six of whom have completed their missions and attained to Buddhahood. The activity of the Spirits of Truth has necessarily been removed from the earthly realm, with the sole exception of their presence "under the bodhi tree" when a Master of Wisdom ascends to Buddhahood. The new Spirit of Truth that Christ would request from the Father, however, would be fundamentally different. Not a danger to mankind's freedom in anyway, this thirteenth Spirit of Truth would abide in the earthly realm. Like Christ Jesus— who expressed His desire to be a friend of man, not a master—the new Spirit of Truth would teach the truth in all things and bring the words of Christ into remembrance (Matthew 14:26). Abiding in the earthly realm, the thirteenth divine bodhisattva would be called *Paraclete*—Comforter, or Advocate. He would bring the baptism by fire and by the Holy Spirit. The new Spirit of Truth would be formed out of the union of three different classes of angels in the third hierarchy. An angel, an archangel or folk soul, and an archai or time spirit would unite to mediate the third member of the Godhead, the Holy Spirit, to mankind. The Comforter would bring divine joy into the human, earthly realm as the free deeds of human beings began to shine with divine love.

Christ Jesus experienced what Buddhism calls Transfiguration (Matthew 17:1-13, Luke 9:28-36). His body began to shine with light and He united with the universe, leaving the cycle of reincarnation behind; yet He transformed His body of light back into its corporeal form for He had not yet finished his earthly task. He completed the stage of the perfection of the human soul (Transfiguration) and then prepared for the next stage which requires the complete spiritualization of the human body (Resurrection). After Passover on Wednesday, Christ Jesus was arrested, brought to trial, found guilty, and sentenced to be crucified. On Good Friday, He was nailed to a cross. On Easter Sunday, He arose from the dead.

As Christianity was entering world history after the turning point of time in 33 A.D., Roman culture had already taken root. Cicero had penned the essays that are still read today by students who wish to learn the Latin language. Livy began what was to become a line of distinguished Roman historians. One hundred years earlier, the greatest poet of ancient times, Virgil, had completed his *Eclogues* and *Georgics* (42-30 B.C.). When Virgil died in 19 B.C., he left instructions in his will that his unpublished epic, *The Aeneid*, be burned. In a very real sense, Caesar Augustus not only ushered in the *Pax Romana* but also founded Roman culture by overruling Virgil's last request. Who else but the emperor of Rome had such authority? *The Aeneid* became a primary focus of study for Latin scholars and has remained so for over two millennia. In its first six books, Virgil achieved a kind of renewal of Homer's *Odyssey*. He continued to explore the Roman character as he had done in his poetry, but his exploration of Aeneas's character allowed him to plumb its depths. In the last six books of the *Aeneid*, he not only completed a renewal of Homer's *Iliad*, but advanced further to unveil a greater mystery. In Aeneas's journey to the Underworld, Virgil revealed the great secret of initiation—the mystery of reincarnation. The father of Aeneas, Anchises, met his son in the Elysian Fields and told him that the Greek and Trojan heroes of the Trojan War would reappear in the earthly realm and come to Rome a millennium later.

Virgil's epic was a literary masterpiece that renewed and reimagined the plot, characters, and literary devices that Homer had once used. Yet it was a lesser-known poem over a century later that served as the true founding epic of Rome. It captured the character of the national leaders and the mission of the folk soul of Rome, much as the later epics of emerging European countries in the Middle Ages, such as *Beowulf* in England, *El Cid* in Spain, or *The Song of Roland* in France had done. Silius Italicus wrote *Punica* around 50 A.D., about 250 years after the Second Punic War. It told about the war between Rome and Carthage and characterized the great leaders: Fabius, Scipio, and Hannibal. Not a renewal of the *Iliad* like Virgil's epic, *Punica* represented a repetition and reversal of it. The action of the epic was not the Greeks attacking Troy, but the Trojans, now reincarnated as the Carthaginians, attacking the Greeks, now reborn as Romans. Hector had become Hannibal and took his revenge on the Romans. Thanks to the greatest historian of ancient times, Plutarch, there are superb biographies of many of these Romans: Fabius, Marcellus, Marcus Cato, and Flaminius. To someone familiar with Homer, it is difficult not to see that their characters coincide with those of Agamemnon, Menelaus, Aeneas, and Paris.

Plutarch (46-120 A.D.) had another role to play in addition to elucidating the characters of the heroes of the Trojan War in their Roman or Carthaginian guise when they reincarnated a millennium later. The great heroes who founded Greece, the first generation of heroes who were extolled in *The Argonautica*, also appear in their Roman incarnation as the founders of the Roman Empire. Pompey, Cicero, Caesar, Brutus, Cato the Younger, and Marc Antony are the reincarnations of Aeetes, Orpheus, Aegeus, Theseus, Pollux, and Heracles. In this connection England's greatest writer, Shakespeare, had something to add. Shakespeare wrote his "Roman" plays and turned Plutarch's biographies into tragedies. In *Julius Caesar* he showed the reincarnated Theseus (i.e., Brutus) opposing the man who had been his father (i.e., Aegeus), who now sought to be king. To uphold his belief in democracy and freedom, Brutus had to stab Caesar.[3] In *Antony and Cleopatra*, the Bard showed Medea still weaving her magic as Cleopatra, and Heracles—now the Roman Antony—showing her the transformative power of love. Antony won a victory over her heart greater than all his triumphs in his battles at the head of Caesar's legions.

Christian communities did exist in the early centuries of the Roman Empire. They were underground and hidden away, especially after the reign of Nero. Murdering the leaders of the Christian movement and torturing their followers in the arenas of Circus Maximus and the Coliseum created a special kind of spiritual evil. A beginning exercise in black magic requires the pupil to enjoy the deaths of the scapegoats. In this case the Christians were were blamed for the homelessness and starvation of the unemployed lower class of Roman society. The communities under attack were the diametrical opposite of the ones to which the Romans belonged. The former were filled with selfless, helpful, and kind people who lived in fear, but believed in love. They were generally uneducated and viewed the Christian god as Apollo. In a certain sense they were right. In the early Christian centuries, Apollo was not active in the cultural realm inspiring the Muses and the creation of literary works, but in the social realm, building these small communities. With the death of Emperor Aurelius in 180 A.D., the Pax Romana came to an end. Within a hundred years, Diocletian divided the empire into two parts. The Western Empire included Europe and was centered in Rome, where the Roman patriarch would gradually achieve hegemony.

The Eastern empire included Eastern Europe, Asia, and Africa and was ruled over by an emperor who continued the policies of the Pax Romana into the Middle Ages. The Eastern Empire also experienced a form of religious awakening in the third century. Mani, the son of a widow, was born around 216 and lived for sixty years. He founded Manichaeism and helped foster a unity of religions. Manichaeism included Buddhism, which extended from India into China via the Silk Road; Zoroastrianism in Persia; and Christianity, which extended from the Near East into Europe. In Europe it took various forms, including the Albigensians and the Cathars. These so-called heresies can be better understood as building blocks for the New Jerusalem and a preparation for the following age of mankind when human beings will have achieved freedom and will wish to join together in the City of Brotherly Love, Philadelphia. The scope of Manichaeism and the intensity and devotion of its adherents point to the activity of the spiritual being that guided Moses out of Egypt and Alexander on his journey to the East. Rudolf Steiner explained that the mysterious union of three different religions by Mani was due to Mani's earlier incarnation as the young man of Nain, also the son of a widow. When the young man of Nain was raised from the dead by Christ Jesus, the forerunner of a new form of initiation was introduced. Steiner viewed Michael, the planetary archangel of the sun, as the archangel of esoteric Christianity and as the explanation for the incredible spread of Manichaeism.

At the beginning of the fourth century, Emperor Constantine brought Christianity out of the darkness and ended the persecution of the Christian communities. In 313, Constantine went to sleep before a great battle that he would fight the following day. He dreamt of how he would win a great victory if he followed the sign of the cross. Putting that sign in front of his army, Constantine won the battle, and, in return, he ordered the persecutions of Christians to cease. The fact that his mother was a practicing Christian also contributed to Constantine's decision to protect Christians from the tortures that they had thus far endured. Constantine shifted the power of the empire further to the east by building a new capital in the city that would bear his name—Constantinople. He gave this power shift a spiritual dimension by ordering that the Palladium residing in the Temple of Vesta should be carried across the seas to the Temple of Sophia in the empire's new capital. Constantinople thus stood at the beginning of a millennium of rulership, while the regency of Rome had come to an end.

In 393, Emperor Theodosius declared Christianity to be the official religion of the empire. The division of the empire by Diocletian was now reflected in the Eastern form of Christianity and the Western form, in Orthodoxy and Catholicism, and in their celebration of Christmas on two different dates. Because of the ever-weakened power of the Western, or Roman emperor, the barbarian invasions of Europe increased, and the population of cities decreased. The Roman patriarch was able to reverse these trends and even, at one point, stand up against the invasion of Atilla the Hun. He became the pope and fortified his position, calling it the Vatican. Scholars gathered to support the movement for a papacy. Saint Augustine (354-430) was the most famous of them, and his *The City of God* extolled the Catholic Church to the point that the authority of the pope was deemed more important than that of Christ. Augustine had been a member of a Manichaeism group before undergoing his conversion to Christianity. For those who might view the victory of Christianity in the Roman Empire as a sign of the weakness of the She-wolf of Rome and its final defeat, the effect of Augustine's attack on Manichaeism should be studied. By branding the Cathars and other groups as heretics, they could then be tortured, murdered, and persecuted as scapegoats just like the early Christians were.

The She-wolf of Rome herself appeared and played an important role in the Old English epic *Beowulf,* which describes events in Northern Europe in the sixth century. The Greek founders had appeared in their first collective incarnation to take part in the quest for the Golden Fleece (*The Argonautica*); the story of their second incarnation as the Roman founders took the stage in Shakespeare's great tragedies (*Julius Caesar* and *Antony and Cleopatra*); and their third incarnation, that of England's founders, is told in *Beowulf.* The English bard identified Grendel's mother as the She-wolf. It is the She-wolf who gave birth to Grendel, the scourge of Hrothgar and of Denmark. If the insight into the character of Theseus can lead to that of Brutus, then the third in the series of incarnations can appear as Hrothgar. The civil war that Antony had unleashed after Caesar's assassination now revealed its spiritual dimension. Antony's call for Ate to release a demon to bring revenge resulted in Grendel's attacks in their next life.[4] Beowulf, however, was strong enough to defeat them both—child and mother. What he could not do was overcome the mighty beast—the great dragon.[5] In slaying the She-wolf, the minion of the great dragon, Beowulf woke the sun demon from his sleep. The strength of Beowulf was of no avail against the beast of the Apocalypse. The dragon returned to his sleep, since the black magic that he hoped to wield needed still to await the time when enough followers could be found to warrant his awakening.

NOTES FOR CHAPTER 3

[1] Octavian taxed the people fairly (based on a census), and he used the money collected to pay for the army, to build the roads, and to provide a postal service and public works projects.

[2] Rudolf Steiner, "The Foundation Stone Meditation." For the author's new translation of the Foundation Stone, see *The Basic Books of Rudolf Steiner*.

[3] "Et tu, Brute. Then fall Caesar." (*Julius Caesar*, Act 3 Scene 2).

[4] *Julius Caesar*, Act 3, scene 9, line 271.

[5] In Raffel's translation of *Beowulf* (1963): for the identification of the She-wolf, see p.73; for the reference to the great dragon, see p.94.

CHAPTER 4:
FEUDAL EUROPE

CONSTANTINE REBUILT THE GREEK CITY OF Byzantium and renamed it Constantinople. In 330 he made it the new capital of the empire. From "New Rome" roads fanned out to the Balkans, to the Middle East, and to North Africa. Its favorable location made it a trading center where silk from China, wheat from Egypt, gems from India, spices from Southeast Asia, and furs from Scandinavia were bought and sold. With the advent of Byzantine emperors and empresses, the city rose to spectacular heights. It combined the bread-and-circuses entertainment of chariot races at the Hippodrome with the architectural marvel of the Church of Hagia Sophia, which was rebuilt by Emperor Justinian in 532 A.D. Justinian is best remembered for his reform of the Roman law. Justinian's Code united the Byzantine empire under his control, influenced both the Roman Catholic Church and medieval monarchs when it reached Western Europe, and even guided modern legal thinkers when they formed the international law in use today.

The attempt of Diocletian in 284 A.D. to save the Roman Empire from collapse by dividing it into two parts—an Eastern and a Western empire—merely postponed the fall of Rome for two centuries. The Byzantine Empire continued to flourish with fair taxation, protection of trade and commerce, and use of proper laws in a civilized society. The Western Empire saw cities dwindle and castles arise to take their place. Their fortifications were surrounded by a moat and a drawbridge. In the attendant villages, the peasantry took up a life of farming. Lords and ladies arose as the nobility to whom the knights and vassals swore fealty. Most of the peasants never traveled more than fifty miles from their place of birth during their lifetime. Feudalism spread over Europe with its kings and dukes, knights and squires, merchants and traders, and illiterate peasantry. Only the Catholic Church provided an education, but it was reserved for their priests and required knowledge of Latin. The Vatican promoted a withdrawal from an active life and supported the building of monasteries and nunneries and the founding of monastic orders like the one established by St. Benedict in 529.

Feudalism in Europe can be compared to the hierarchical structure of ancient Egyptian society and its pyramidal shape. The advances in Greece and Rome in developing democratic and republican forms of government gave way to a completely autocratic form of government in the Byzantine empire and the dualistic autocracies of secular kings and a religious pope in Europe. The Byzantine form of autocracy made the emperor the head of the Orthodox Church as well since he appointed the patriarchs. The Roman patriarch (the Pope) would not accept subservience to the Byzantine emperor, and thus the seeds were laid for the schism that finally took place in the eleventh century between Orthodoxy and Catholicism. The deep irony of the schism involved the fact that the Byzantine emperor had played a major role in defending Europe from the rising tide of Islam in the Near East. By the eleventh century the Moslem religion had expanded eastward into India and westward across North Africa. Only the strategic location of Constantinople and the heroism of the Byzantine army kept Islam at bay. Despite the terms of the schism going into effect, the Byzantine emperor obtained the Pope's help in fighting the Muslim armies. The Pope issued a call to defend the Holy Land and worked with European monarchs to raise soldiers for a Crusade—the first of many as it would turn out. Declaring each other anathema and then having Orthodoxy and Catholicism join in a Holy War in the name of the God of Love against a third religion suggests that religious intolerance has swallowed them all. The attack on Manichaeism stood at the beginning of a process that came to include crusades against Islam, a schism with

Orthodoxy, and Inquisitions against the Knights Templar in the 1300s and Protestantism in the 1500s.

Historians have identified the forces leading to the downfall of Rome with the She-wolf's activity in the "bread and circuses" offered to the Roman mobs and, secondly, in the advent of the "evil emperors." They should also notice her continued activity in the attempt of Catholicism to stamp out heresies and carry out Crusades and Inquisitions. The She-wolf failed to gain a foothold in Northern Europe as described in the epic of *Beowulf* when Grendel's mother fell before the hero of the Geats. Hatred and bloodlust are the ABCs of black magic and the pathway which the minion of the great dragon would have her adherents follow. Augustine played a major role in bringing this eventuality to pass. In 406 he wrote *The City of God*—a kind of caricature of the New Jerusalem—and he stated, "I would not accept the teachings of Christ if they were not founded on the authority of the church." Since Augustine's theological book is the principal work of early Roman Catholicism, the pope, and by extension, the opinions of Augustine justify any persecution carried out in their name.

The Roman Catholic Church did not take much interest in a significant stream of philosophy that emerged in the early Christian centuries. Neo-Platonism involved a mystical approach to what thinkers like Philo and Plotinus called "The Intellect." Another renewal of Platonism occurred in the eleventh and twelfth centuries in France. The School of Chartres required its members to take up the study of the trivium and the quadrivium—the Seven Liberal Arts. While their work took place in the environs of the Chartres cathedral, their influence spread throughout Europe. In England, John of Salisbury penned his treatise on the first liberal art, Grammatica.

In the Eastern world in the schools of philosophy that Alexander the Great had founded, Aristotelianism continued to be studied. With the advent of Mohammed in the seventh century, the influence of Islam on Aristotle's philosophy began to be felt. A kind of Arabism was formed that reached its zenith in the ninth century in the court of Haroun al-Rashid in Baghdad. When it was introduced into Europe two centuries later, neither the Church Fathers nor the Neo-Platonists could offer much resistance to the arguments of Arab scholars such as Averroes. The development of Scholasticism in Paris at the beginning of the thirteenth century, however, showed that a Christian theology could be built on an Aristotelian basis. Albertus Magnus helped the efforts to shape a new theology with his lectures and treatises and began to create what became the University of Paris.

It was Thomas Aquinas's entrance into the fray that enabled Christian theology to triumph over the Islamic theology of Averroes and won Thomas Aquinas the title of Defender of the Faith. Aquinas's most famous work, the *Summa Theologica*, remains the classic of Christian theology. The title given to Aquinas for that accomplishment was Doctor Angelicus. When Aquinas wanted to write about Aristotle in the *Summa*, he always called him the Philosopher. He was trying to make clear that he (Aquinas) believed that Aristotle was the founder of philosophy and that he (Aquinas) had a different relationship to Aristotle than anyone else could have—that he (Aquinas) was the reincarnated Aristotle.[1] As the founder of philosophy it was particularly his task or mission to make any corrections necessary to ensure that the advance of philosophy down through the ages would not change philosophy into a caricature—or even worse, the opposite—of itself. In simplest terms Aquinas needed to align Aristotelianism with the advent of the Christ. Scholasticism allowed the intellect to mature in the age when its development was of paramount importance. Thinking logically could then be able to unite with active thinking in the age of freedom.

Michael, the archangel of the sun, had been the guiding spirit of the Exodus from Egypt, of Alexander the Great's journey to the East, and of the spread of Manichaeism from China to the Straits of Gibraltar. In feudal Europe, Michael became the archangel of esoteric Christianity, the spirit guide behind the rise of the Grail knights. The epic poem of Wolfram von

Eschenbach, *Parzival*, told of how the knight Parzival became the Lord of the Grail in 869. *Parzival* also presented the attentive reader a pathway to the spirit world in the trials and tribulations of the son of the widow who travelled from foolishness through doubt to blessedness. This poem is like that of the *Bhagavad-Gita* in that daily meditation on its content provides something like a dictionary of the people and events in one's everyday life. Walter Stein in his masterpiece, *The Ninth Century in the Light of the Holy Grail*, explained how the eightfold path of Gautama Buddha was embedded in its sixteen chapters. Equally astounding, the 827 sections of *Parzival* can be arranged in the form of a plot pyramid and a deeper meaning of any section can be discovered by examining its corresponding section on the opposite side.

Parzival's adventure began when he left his mother and his home to visit King Arthur's court. In the first stage of his development, Parzival was the fool. Herzeleid, his mother, had even dressed him in a jester's outfit. During his arrival in King Arthur's encampment, Parzival was seen by Lady Cunneware, she who was never to laugh until she beheld him who was to win supreme honor. Then her mouth burst forth laughing, and Antanor, her brother who was never to speak a word unless she laughed, also began to speak. Sir Kay took offense at their prophecy of supreme honor for a strapping youth who looked and acted like a fool. He thrashed them both for belittling Arthur's court. When Parzival returned some time later to try for a second time to become a knight of the Round Table, he was helped immensely by Sir Gawain. When a representative of the Grail knights spoke in opposition to Parzival's request, Parzival's entrance into the Round Table was denied. Parzival moved into the background, and Gawain supplanted him as the principal character. Parzival was still very active, though only an attentive reader such as Walter Stein could clearly discern it. The events surrounding Gawain's journey to Castle Marvel, and his trials and tribulations there, described his heroic stand against the actual misuse of magical powers by a black magician. Stein's research into Landulf II, Duke of Capua, showed the historical figure who had been depicted as Klingsor, the ruler of Castle Marvel. Klingsor himself was a minion, a servant of the She-wolf of Rome who had previously directed Herod's efforts to prevent the birth of the Messiah. Now the She-wolf hoped to prevent the opening of the gate to the Grail Castle and the laying of the first foundation stone of the New Jerusalem. She hoped to thwart Parzival by attacking Sir Gawain. She used the wonder bed and the wreath of virtue to enmesh Sir Gawain in a duel with Grammoflanz, but Parzival averted the near-certain tragedy.

Parzival faced a more difficult challenge when he fought Feirefiz, the leader of the Muslim armies. Feirefiz was noble. He defeated Parzival in a duel but refused to take his life without first learning the name of the opponent who had fought against him so valiantly. When Parzival finally identified himself, the two half-brothers who shared a common sire—Gahmuret—put away their enmity. The revelation that Feirefiz was his brother also enabled Parzival to take part in the ritual of the Grail since becoming the Lord of the Grail required him to bring his brother to the ceremony. Feirefiz, despite his belief in Islam, attended the ceremony and experienced good fortune. He met the Grail-bearer, Parzival's aunt, Repanse de Schoye, and fell in love with her. He married her before returning to the East. The ceremony with the chalice in the Grail Castle in 869 marked the beginning of Parzival's service as Lord of the Grail. It also signified the laying of the first foundation stone of the New Jerusalem. The stone of jasper was made of the same substance as the cup that Solomon had once received from the Queen of Sheba, that had been used to serve the disciples on Passover, and that contained the blood that Christ had spilled while He was being crucified. Thus was the first gate of the Grail Castle opened by the Grail knights to the whole world. The Arthurian knights would discover when they set forth on their quest for the Holy Grail that they must give up strife in order to win the Grail. Some knights like Sir Gawain were able to achieve this ideal.

The second stream of esoteric Christianity that became active in the Middle Ages was led by Lazarus/John. Just as the young man of Nain had been raised from the dead by Christ Jesus and prepared for his role as the initiate who would found the first gate to the heavenly home of New Jerusalem, so had Lazarus been raised from the dead by Christ Jesus and prepared for his role in founding the second gate. Wolfram von Eschenbach's epic told of the path that Parzival had to tread. A book written in 1603 by Johannes Valentine told of another path to the Grail Castle. *The Alchymical Wedding of Christian Rosenkreutz* was written by amanuensis (automatic writing), and Rosenkreutz himself was the true author of the story of his own initiation in 1459. The laying of the second foundation stone—the philosopher's stone or the stone of the wise—also opened a new path of initiation to those who wished to enter the home of the bodhisattvas and the spiritual world of Providence. Like the path of the Grail knights, this path required the guidance of a master. Rosenkreutz established small groups of pupils who were hidden away from public view. Having undergone such training, his pupils, in turn, took on the task of forming small, secret groups and extending the number of initiates able to enter the holy realm of the Grail.[2]

NOTES FOR CHAPTER 4

[1] See Bockholt, *Rudolf Steiner and the Mission of Ita Wegman.*

[2] See Lievegoed, *The Battle for the Soul.*

CHAPTER 5:
THE CENTRAL EUROPEAN AGE

THE ACTIVITY OF MICHAEL IN MANICHAEISM, the Grail stream, and Rosicrucianism led Rudolf Steiner to name Michael the archangel of esoteric Christianity. In a similar way the historians characterized the activity of Apollo in the opening of the new age of freedom as the Renaissance, the Elizabethan Age, and neoclassicism, i.e., the rebirth of Apollonian culture, the renewal of Greek tragedy, and the new classical culture. Apollo was especially active in the Italian masters, the three painters who epitomized the Renaissance. Leonardo da Vinci, Michelangelo, and Raphael lived from 1452 to 1564. If Steiner's research on the past lives of these great artists is brought to mind, then the activity of Apollo can be more clearly articulated. Steiner suggested that these painters could be viewed as reincarnations of Christ's disciples. Since Apollo was the avatar of Christ, his memories of Christ's words and deeds are preserved in him in a special way. The inspirations that Apollo as the spirit of Catholicism brought to the Italian masters came forth as works of art, revelations of the life of Christ, and living proof of the entrance of the God of Love onto the earthly plane. Their masterpieces extended into the realm of sculpture with Michelangelo's statues of "David" and the "Pieta." Michelangelo's past life as Peter brought the activity of Catholicism to a kind of culmination with his creation of the dome of St. Peter's Cathedral in 1564.

The further development of Apollo as the spirit of the Renaissance required his emergence from the Vatican and his northward journey from Rome into the Netherlands. Rembrandt (1606-1669) was able to carry painting to new heights. His Biblical scenes were as powerful and drenched in reality as those of the Italian masters. The influence of Apollo as the spirit of the Renaissance was supplemented in Rembrandt's other paintings by the inspiration of the master of Christian esotericism who founded Rosicrucianism. Rembrandt's paintings of common people living everyday lives were as dynamic and real as his religious paintings, and people viewing them cannot but feel them coming alive in a spiritual atmosphere of utter beauty. His picture of a knight on horseback is perhaps the best evidence of this Rosicrucian influence. Rudolf Steiner suggested that Christian Rosenkreutz himself was the subject of this painting.

When the Renaissance entered England, it was called the Elizabethan Age. Because it contained England's greatest writer, it was also named the

Shakespearean Age. Some literary critics even questioned Shakespeare's actual existence since his grasp of so many different fields of knowledge was so extensive and so deep. Many said that he must have been Sir Francis Bacon, the founder of a school of philosophy (the British empiricists) and the greatest scholar of his time. Rudolf Steiner's research into this question acknowledged Shakespeare's lack of a scholastic education as raising the question of the source of his understanding of so many and so diverse branches of the tree of knowledge. Steiner did suggest, however, that an inspiring spirit, the same one who had worked with Rembrandt, could have assisted Shakespeare. The influence of Christian Rosenkreutz is especially apparent in Shakespeare's tragedies, which demonstrate how the modern age magically transformed Brutus—the arch-villain who murdered Julius Caesar and who was being devoured by Lucifer in the lowest circle of the Inferno—into "the most noble Roman of them all." So too did the Bard transmute Marc Antony's biography by Plutarch into the tragedy of *Antony and Cleopatra*, the tragedy of last love. Both plays were discussed in chapter two, "Ancient Greece," in relation to the reincarnation of the founders of ancient Greece who then became the founders of the Roman Empire.

Shakespeare's foremost play, *Hamlet*, is also the greatest literary work in the English language. Shakespeare can be compared to Homer, Virgil, Dante, and

Goethe, and to no others. His *Hamlet* built on what Homer had accomplished in *The Iliad* and what Italicus had brought to life in *Punica* to reveal a third incarnation of the Greek and Trojan heroes in the battle between Norway and Denmark. In the castle of Elsinore, William Shakespeare brought the Trojan War onto the stage. Rudolf Steiner's research on Hamlet as the reborn Hector can be explored in great detail.[1] Shakespeare's other tragedies—*King Lear*, *Othello*, *Macbeth*, and *Romeo and Juliet*—are certainly comparable to any that the Greek tragedians produced. His histories and comedies swelled his literary output to thirty-six plays, and their success in withstanding the test of time mark Shakespeare as the world's greatest dramatist.

The influence of the English Renaissance did not cease with the deaths of Queen Elizabeth the First and William Shakespeare. With the passage of about a century, the Apollonian influence in culture began to be called neo-classicism. A rebirth of classical ideals in English literature occurred in John Locke's essays and in the poetry of Alexander Pope and John Dryden. By the middle of the eighteenth century, it had crossed the Atlantic Ocean and was entering America, especially in the works of Thomas Jefferson.[2] The Rosicrucian influence, when combined with the Apollonian influence, tends to awaken Classical ideals and bring them alive in the new age of freedom. In neoclassic architecture and sculpture, the glory of Athens and the grandeur of Rome was not just remembered, but, like the Capitol Building, it was hallowed by Masonic rituals led by George Washington so that it might become the Temple of Liberty.

The leading time spirit who would usher in the new age of freedom did not become active until 1517 when Martin Luther posted his *Ninety-five Theses* on a church door in the town of Wittenberg, Germany. Luther's opposition to the sale of indulgences led to the beginning of the Reformation and the activity of the spirit of Protestantism. This spirit of the age ruled as an archai, and when the Roman Catholic pope used his authority to try and silence Luther, Luther championed human freedom. The presence of the conscience, the voice of God in the human soul, was above the authority of the Church. Luther's idea of one's vocation as a calling of God was just as revolutionary. The need for free human beings to take an active role in modern life and embrace their calling signaled a reversal of the medieval tendency to withdraw from the world and enter a cloister or monastery. Luther even concluded that priests should lead a normal life and marry and raise a family.

John Calvin extended Luther's idea of human freedom even further. He believed that every member of a church had the right to read the Bible and interpret it, and not have Biblical passages read to them in

Latin and be told their meaning by a priest. Calvin supported the efforts to translate the Bible into one's native tongue and to fund public education so that people would become literate and could read Scripture by themselves. He also viewed wealth differently than the Catholic Church. Rather than condemning money as a sign of worldliness and as sinful, he suggested that it was a sign of God's approval. In his book *The Protestant Ethic and the Spirit of Capitalism,* Weber pointed out how encouraging public education, literacy, and the amassing of wealth helped capitalism thrive in those countries that became Protestant. Calvin's view of pre-destination, however, worked contrary to his efforts to bring freedom into the modern world. By arguing that man's view of his freedom was faulty and that man's efforts to lead a good life could not change what God had preordained—i.e., rising into heaven or falling into hell—the false idea of being one of the elect was promoted. Rather than recognizing that all men are created equal, a belief in one's superiority was encouraged, and non-believers could be looked down on. The fact that pre-destination completely contradicts human freedom is why Calvinism can seem like an attempt to replace the Pope's authority with illogic.

John Knox in Scotland helped Protestantism by providing its churches with a less hierarchical form. He organized local churches led by presbyters or elders and called their form of governance Presbyterianism. In

England, John Wesley put an emphasis on self-development exercises for church members as the name that he chose for this form of Protestantism suggested—Methodist. He also emphasized the importance of social involvement and the need to follow Christ's example. He organized the church year into a series of eight seasons and suggested that certain Biblical passages be assigned to each of the seasons so that the cycle of the year would mirror the events in the life of Christ. The Protestant denominations that emerged from 1517 to 1750 included Lutheranism in Germany and Scandinavia, Calvinism in the Netherlands and Switzerland, Presbyterianism in Scotland, and Methodism in England. The Spirit of Protestantism essentially encompassed Northern Europe and Great Britain.

Certain English kings seemed to resemble the evil emperors of Rome. Shakespeare's *Richard III* revealed how selfish and heartless the king who ruled over England from 1483 to 1485 truly was. Henry VIII who ruled from 1509 to 1547 was even worse. His successive murders of his seven wives finally forced the Pope himself to intervene. When Henry VIII ignored the Pope's threat of excommunication and the Pope carried through with it, Henry VIII simply formed his own church. Like the emperors of the Eastern empire, he placed himself at the head of the Church of England and called his new religion Episcopalianism and warned the remaining Catholic Churches not to interfere with his government. With Henry VIII's death, the sole remaining heir to the throne was Elizabeth. She was able to work with Parliament and maintained political freedom during England's Renaissance. Her defeat of the Spanish Armada in 1588 foreshadowed the superiority the British navy would come to enjoy.

The death of Queen Elizabeth in 1603 caused great difficulty since she left no heirs. The king of Scotland was asked to join England and Scotland together, and he became the king of Great Britain, King James I. He had been active in the circles of Scottish Freemasonry, and he brought with him a plan for how to attain British leadership in the new age.[3] The plan contained two parts, with a transition period between the two. The first part involved a repetition of the creation of the Roman Empire in the previous age. The second part required establishing a cultural hegemony like that attained by Roman Catholicism over Europe in the Middle Ages. The one-sidedness of the plan of the Western secret societies is shown by its omission of the development of ancient Greek culture. The difficulty of the transition between parts one and two would be exacerbated by the omission of Greek culture since the culture of the new age of freedom includes the Renaissance and its development into neoclassicism.

James I worked with the shipbuilders, the merchants who needed warehouses, the Anglican leaders, and the British navy who would guard the shipping lanes. By 1619 the first ship of slaves arrived in Jamestown, and the plan began to come together. Charles I took over after James's death in 1625, and he continued to give shape to the colonial empire that James I had envisioned. His autocratic tendencies won out, however, and he faced opposition from both Parliament and the group of Protestants who wanted to purify the Church of England, the Puritans. The Puritan leader, Oliver Cromwell, formed a regiment into a "church," and the New Model Army took to the field in 1644. By 1648 Cromwell had defeated the Scottish army, and the following year he became the leader of the Protectorate. He beheaded King Charles I and refused to support the shipbuilders or build warehouses for trade. While it seemed that Cromwell had destroyed the plan of King James I, the lords of Parliament, the Anglican Church leaders, and the businessman who had engaged in world trade did have to adjust, but they remained under the sway of the Western secret societies and held to their belief in Anglo-Saxon superiority.

The Restoration of the monarchy took place in 1660, and King Charles II remained king until 1685. The slave trade resumed and in the next one hundred years over two million Africans were loaded onto boats at the beginning of what was called the Middle Passage. The economic aspect of James I's plan was called "the golden triangle." It involved ships being loaded with clothes from the textile manufacturing companies in England and traveling to the west coast of Africa where the clothes were sold, and slaves were purchased. The conditions that the slaves endured were sufficiently harsh that the an estimated twenty-five percent of them perished in the Middle Passage to the Caribbean Islands and the American colonies. Five hundred thousand slaves died, and the Episcopalian leaders successfully carried out their role of hiding what they could and justifying what they couldn't. They even succeeded in drawing a color line by getting laws passed that helped engrain the idea of black inferiority in the minds of generations down to the present day. The third leg of the golden triangle involved selling slaves and making a huge profit. The slavers then purchased cotton which was loaded onto the ships and brought back to England to be spun into clothes to sell in Africa.

The British sailors who manned the slave ships had to be of a certain type. They had to believe that the deaths they were causing were somehow right and good. The bread and circuses of Rome with their torture of Christians and feeding them to the lions can be seen as training grounds for the torture and murder that the slave trader would embrace. Nor did the lives of the black men and women who survived the Middle Passage look any different than the lives of their brothers and sisters who had perished. The system of slavery set up in the American colonies was based on white supremacy, the humiliation of black people, the torture of anyone opposing it, and murder, often with tar-n-feathering or a lynching.

NOTES FOR CHAPTER 5

[1] See Spaulding, *The Parzival Mystery Stream*, pp. 32-40.

[2] The author discusses the influence of the Count of St. Germain, a later reincarnation of Rosenkreutz, on both Benjamin Franklin and Jefferson in his book *A Sanctuary for the Rights of Mankind: The Founding Fathers and the Temple of Liberty*.

[3] See Steiner's *The Karma of Untruthfulness* and Spaulding's *The Prophecy of Oz* pp. 51-52.

CHAPTER 6:
THE AGE OF FREEDOM

FOR EMERSON, THE SPIRIT GUIDE OF AMERICA, the significance of the "Declaration of Independence" in 1776 could be discovered by relating it to the year 776 B.C. and the inauguration of the Olympic Games in ancient Greece. The founding of the culture of ancient Greece was reflected in the birth of the American Republic. The Founding Fathers themselves looked up to George Washington as first in war for his defeat of the British army and as first in peace for his twice unanimous election to the office of President and as first in the hearts of his countrymen for his service as President of the Constitutional Convention and his disbanding of the Continental Army. His spiritual activity in the Freemasonic Lodges of his time is lesser known. The Masonic activities of the other Founding Father who was deemed to be Washington's equal are quite famous especially during the time of Franklin's negotiations in 1785 with Great Britain on a peace treaty, the Treaty of Paris, when he was said to have achieved his apotheosis. Franklin's subsequent return

to America and his activity in unifying the delegates
to the Constitutional Convention is often credited for
the successful adoption of the Constitution in 1787.
The architect of the Constitution itself, however, was
James Madison. The man responsible for transmuting
its ideas and principles into the Freemasonic principles
of architecture was Thomas Jefferson.

Congress approved the construction of the Capitol Building, and the first part of a much larger plan
began to unfold. George Washington spent much of
the three years of his retirement working on this plan
which was then called "Washington, in the Territory
of Columbia." Phylis Wheatley's poem, "To His Excel-
lency General Washington," written in 1775, prophesied
his victory over the British army. Her poem explained
that Washington's service and loyalty to the goddess
Columbia would be the spiritual basis for his victory
over Britannia. The Capitol Building envisioned by
Jefferson was the transformation of the Constitution
of the United States into an architectural form, a Free-
mason temple dedicated to Columbia and given the
name of the Temple of Liberty. Even today, the statue
that stands atop the dome of the Capital Building can
remind people that she is but a representation of that
spiritual being whose activity in the Temple of Liberty
imparted spiritual guidance to America. She it was
who inspired the Founding Fathers in the Revolutionary War and the Abolitionists in the Civil War.[1]

A fuller vision of this "sanctuary for the rights of mankind" would reveal the three pillars of the Temple of Liberty. The L'Enfant plan that Washington had hoped to improve upon placed what is today the Mall in a direct relationship to the three pillars of wisdom, beauty, and strength and to the three houses of the zodiac. Washington did not agree with L'Enfant's idea of an equestrian statue at the center of the diamond-shaped form of the Mall. Many years later, an Egyptian obelisk was chosen as the appropriate way to honor George Washington. The Washington Monument points to ancient Egypt and the pillar of wisdom. The final two additions to the Washington Mall, the memorials to Lincoln and to Jefferson, also clearly point to the pillar that they represent. The Lincoln Memorial finds its model in the Parthenon, the temple to Athena, and it points to ancient Greece, the pillar of beauty. The Jefferson Memorial was modeled on the Pantheon, the temple to all the gods, and it points to ancient Rome, the pillar of strength.

From one point of view the mission of America's Founding Fathers can be characterized as enshrining freedom in the Temple of Liberty, with some of the Founders in favor and others opposed. In the case of Thomas Paine, this mission was expressed in more stark terms as the end of kingship. Benjamin Franklin served as a representative and spokesman for the American colonies. During his extensive stay in Great Britain, he met Paine, an Englishman, and convinced him to travel to Pennsylvania and serve as editor of Franklin's "Pennsylvania Gazette." Paine helped Phylis Wheatley publish her poem, and he inspired Americans to fight for their independence by writing essays for "The Crisis." Even after the defeat of the Redcoats, Paine's objective was not fulfilled. He journeyed to France and wrote *The Rights of Man* to support the French Revolution and help to unseat the King. His past lives as Jason and Octavian reveal him as leader of the Argonauts and the first Roman emperor, and as an opponent of Hercules/Antony and Medea/ Cleopatra. In an important way Paine aided his erstwhile enemies, and he also faced up to the daunting task that destiny had provided him. As Caesar Augustus, Paine had ushered the idea of kingship onto the stage of world history. The Pax Romana showed that it could be a step forward in social development. But in the Age of Freedom, King George III and King Louis XVI were, if not as bad as the evil emperors, yet as incompetent and mentally unstable as could be possibly imagined. What the Founding Fathers did offer was an alternative to autocracy, with the idea of an executive branch of government and the office of a President elected by the people. While it was not a full answer to the question of kingship that Paine had raised, it was a serious beginning.

The second Revolutionary War is not discussed as such in history textbooks. Instead, it is called "the War of 1812" and its actual significance is largely ignored. As Hegel correctly surmised, a world historic idea must appear twice on the stage of world history: first as an event, and secondly as proof that the first time was not an accidental happenstance. The example Hegel chose was from Roman history: the rise of Julius Caesar to kingship and, following his assassination, the elevation of Caesar Augustus. Since Octavian accomplished the latter deed, it fell to Thomas Paine to bring the ruler-ship of kings to its proper end. The greatness of his first deed and of the Pax Romana should not dim the luster of his contributions to ending an idea that had outlived its usefulness. It is interesting to note that Hegel did not recognize Washington's victory at Yorktown and the founding of the American republic as a significant historical event, nor did he realize that when Great Britain attacked America a second time and lost a second time, that a repetition of the first event had occurred. The British rulers and the leadership of the Western secret societies, however, knew full well what they were doing. The problem was not that they didn't know that the spiritual being, Britannia, had served in ancient times as the time spirit of Rome. The problem was that they only wanted to use this knowledge to benefit themselves.[2] They believed that the rest of humanity would have to endure second class citizenship or, in the case of black people, slavery. Just as the She-wolf of Rome, the emissary of the Great Beast of the Apocalypse, had stood behind the slaughter of the innocents by Herod and the torture of Christians by Nero, so did she inspire a direct assault on those Freemasons who had hoped to enshrine Freedom in the Temple Liberty. The British army attacked the home of this temple in Washington, D.C., and burned the Capitol Building to the ground.

In 1819, Congress passed a law that showed just how successful the British attack had been. The Missouri Comprise installed slavery as a legacy of the Founding Fathers. Franklin had led the Founders in their opposition to slavery by establishing an anti-slavery society and attempting to raise the issue in Congress in 1790. His death the following year meant that the one Founder with the gravitas of Washington and with the strength of Beowulf, who had himself opposed the She-wolf and defeated her, could not expose the decadence of the Western secret societies and the evil of white supremacy which threatened to undermine the U.S. Constitution and the ideal of freedom it was intended to bring to all people.

In 1860 the party of slavery and the newly formed anti-slavery party, the Democratic and the Republican parties, nominated Breckinridge and Abraham Lincoln for President. Lincoln's victory led to a civil war. The slavery party had no real problem with the torture and bloodshed that would ensue from a great civil war. The slave owners had the same in store for their chattel anyway. Nor did the defeat of the Confederacy of Jefferson Davis and Lee's Army of Northern Virginia change the minds of Southerners to help them accept the inalienable truth that all men are created equal. In the very year of General Robert E. Lee's surrender at Appomattox, the Ku Klux Klan came out of hiding and vehemently opposed the idea of Reconstruction. By 1876, these wizards of torture and lynching had achieved the Hayes Compromise. The Union Army completed its withdrawal from the Southern States and the new form of slavery, segregation, descended on the South and, along with it, the color line in the form of the Jim Crow laws.

A new form of spiritual activity became visible in the cultural realm of Europe about the same time that Columbia, the guiding spirit of America, became manifest in the political realm through the Founding Fathers. Just as Roman Catholicism became active in the fine arts and in literature as the spirit of the Renaissance, so did Protestantism transform into the spirit of idealism around the year 1750. The essays of Lessing and Herder in German literature inaugurated this cultural movement. The dramas of Schiller gained it an even greater following. Unfortunately, they also brought Schiller to the attention of the Western secret societies. Goethe, Schiller's best friend and Idealism's greatest exponent, believed Schiller's death was an assassination, as was probably also the case for Mozart.

Goethe's poetry gained him fame, but *Faust*, his masterwork which he finished on his deathbed in 1832, became the Bible of the German soldiers who carried it in their knapsacks in World War I.

A philosophical movement also emerged in Germany during the time of Schiller and Goethe. It too was called Idealism, and it included Germany's best philosophers: Fichte, Hegel, and Schelling. They looked at the question of freedom from the point of view of pure thinking. Schilling's work at the turn of the eighteenth century, *Of Human Freedom*, showed that a fully self-conscious and active thinking could freely choose the ideal it would seek to attain and work towards its realization. The height and breadth of Hegel's philosophical output rivals that of Plato and Aristotle. It is the reason that many philosophers view the appearance of German Idealism as the modern counterpart of the Academy and the Lyceum in ancient Athens.

Just as the Renaissance, after its appearance in the Italian Masters, began to move north and enter England in the Elizabethan Age, so did German Idealism, migrate to Great Britain where it was called Romanticism. With the publication of *Lyrical Ballads* in 1798, for the first time in history, a literary movement was formally announced as such to the public. William Wordsworth and Samuel Coleridge collaborated in a fashion similar to that of Goethe and Schiller. They brought the spiritual beauty of common people and everyday life into modern poetry and joined it with the glory of imaginative visions made accessible using commonplace poetic expressions. Other poets such as Lord Byron and Shelley joined the literary movement of Romanticism along with a group of novelists, including Jane Austin, the Brontë sisters, and Sir Walter Scott. In a country where poet laureate has long been an actual office held by a living poet, it must be noted that most literary critics consider John Keats to be England's greatest poet. A good friend of Shelley, Keats had completed his poetic output by the age of twenty-five, and it has stood at the pinnacle of the poems of Romanticism ever since. Keats and his fellow Romantic poets brought the development of English literature begun by *Beowulf* to its fitting conclusion. Goethe accomplished a similar deed for German literature's development since the time of *Parzival* in the thirteenth century with the completion of *Faust* in 1832.

Idealism had not yet completed its mission with the activity of Hegel and Goethe in Germany and of Wordsworth and Keats in England. It journeyed over the Atlantic Ocean, as the neoclassic Renaissance had once done, and entered the two American essayists who would take up the beginning of American literature created by Jefferson's essays. Emerson and Thoreau collaborated as their German and English counterparts had once done, and *Walden* was the outcome. They joined forces with two other budding writers, Margaret Fuller and Bronson Alcott, and formed the Concord Circle. In their meetings they called their hometown of Concord by the name of "Little Weimar." They recognized that their efforts were but minor literary works in comparison to those of Goethe, the mastermind of the German people, in his hometown of Weimar. Idealism had to change its name once again. Emerson gave the name to what he described as "Idealism as it appears in America": Transcendentalism.

Although the essays of Emerson and Thoreau may seem minor in such august company, they do have a special significance which may not be easily recognized. Like the essays of Cicero in Roman literature, they stand at the beginning of a national literature. The history of America began with Jefferson's "Declaration of Independence." If Emerson and Thoreau hoped to found a national literature in tune with the spirit of Freedom enshrined in the Temple of Liberty, then their essays would have to awaken the human mind to active thinking, the only true foundation for a free deed. The spirit of the Central European age, Idealism, had inspired the essayists, poets, dramatists, novelists, and philosophers in Germany, England, and America to lay the foundation for free people to take up active thinking. Its withdrawal in 1850 hit Emerson especially hard. He wondered if he would ever write again, but he proved more than capable.[3]

Great Britain viewed the loss of the American colonies as an apparent disaster which threw their plan of building an empire into disarray. A book published by Adam Smith in 1776, *The Wealth of Nations*, promoted an economic system that would enrich the mother country and keep her colonies subservient, even as, the self-same year, "The Declaration of Independence" announced the willingness of Americans to break away from the monarchy and take up a new form of government that embodied the self-evident rights of man in the age of freedom. The unwillingness of the American colonists to accept the accoutrements of mercantilism—for example the tea tax—implied that other colonies like Canada, Australia, and India might also rebel. British merchants were surprised that, rather than rebelling, the other colonies seemed happy to continue trading with their mother country under the policy of *laissez-faire*, which helped turn the golden triangle of the slave trade into the engine of the industrial revolution. The colonies shipped their raw materials to England where the new factories in Manchester and elsewhere provided the finished goods to be shipped back to the colonies.

Since the British navy ruled the seven seas, British merchant vessels were under its protection and found little difficulty in expanding their trade with all other countries. This boost to trade capitalism was also aided by Britain's use of the gold standard in business transactions. Great Britain spent much time and effort in amassing a large gold reserve to manipulate the business transactions of their merchants in their favor. The French Revolution threatened to hinder the further development of the British empire. The torture and execution of the French nobility gave way to the rise of Napoleon. The first great battle with France occurred at sea and cost Britain its best sea captain. Admiral Nelson lost his life, but not before he won the Battle at Trafalgar in 1805 and halted the French attempt to invade England. Another decade had to pass before Napoleon met his final defeat at the hands of General Wellington at the Battle of Waterloo. France's loss of political hegemony in Europe, however, did not prevent the French from playing a major role in the further development of capitalism. By the middle of the nineteenth century, the French banking system had expanded and become the leader in the development of loan capitalism.

Great Britain continued to expand its empire, even as it began to grant its English-speaking colonies a measure of self-government. This growth especially occurred under the reign of Queen Victoria from 1837 to 1901. When she took on the title of Empress of India, she showed a willingness to use the British army to suppress any opposition to her rulership. In 1839, Queen Victoria even made use of more extreme measures when she declared war on China for refusing to allow British ships to bring opium to its country. With

British doctors telling the public that opium is no more dangerous than tea, the Queen carried out the Opium War and flooded China with drugs.

By the end of the nineteenth century, industrial capitalism began to reach a certain height in Germany and in the United States with the Robber Barons. The interweaving of the production of goods and their distribution among the many nations led at last to a world economy. This outcome was considered unacceptable by the Western secret societies. They viewed a single world economy meeting the needs of all people as the end of competition and, even worse, the end of the growth of profits.[4] The Western secret societies decided to get rid of the conundrum posed by the world economy by bringing the first part of its plan for world domination—a repetition of the Roman Empire by building a British empire—to an end. Even as early as the 1890s, these occult groups began offering up ideas of how to bring about the transition to the second part of the plan—a repetition of Roman Catholicism in feudal Europe—by building a highly technological and commercial culture and employing the genius of the Anglo-Saxon sub-race to exploit sub-earthly forces for their own benefit.

CHAPTER SIX NOTES

1 See Spaulding, *A Sanctuary for the Rights of Mankind.*

2 In Freemasonic meetings, they referred to themselves as the Anglo-Saxon sub-race.

3 See York and Spaulding, *Ralph Waldo Emerson: the Infinitude of the Private Man.*

4 See Rudolf Steiner, *The Karma of Untruthfulness.*

CHAPTER 7:
THE AGE OF LIGHT

THE NEW SUN REGENCY, IN A CERTAIN SENSE, represented the return—after the passage of 2190 years—of the sun regency of Michael in the time of ancient Greece. It was prepared for by the publications of the essays of Ralph Waldo Emerson and the religious discourses and philosophical reflections of Soren Kierkegaard. The opening of the sun regency in 1879 coincided with the completion of Friedrich Nietzsche's *Thus Spake Zarathustra*. Rudolf Steiner later wrote *Friedrich Nietzsche: A Fighter for Freedom* to defend the "early Nietzsche" from the misinterpretations and slanders that the illness of the "later Nietzsche" had given rise to. In 1894, Rudolf Steiner published his seminal philosophical work, *The Philosophy of Freedom*.[1] It answered the basic question of modern philosophy fully and completely. It showed the advance that Philosophia had made since the age of Michael's rulership in ancient Greece and the time of the revelations of Plato's *Dialogues* and Aristotle's philosophy. Philosophia had risen from the rank of angel to become the planetary archangel of the sun in order to continue the sun regency in the age of freedom in a special way. Rudolf Steiner tried to clarify the significance of his first basic book by saying that it differed from the other basic books and from his six thousand lectures because it would stand the test of time. It would provide future generations a millennium from its publication the insight and inspiration they would need to master the soul trial of our age and attain to the sphere of freedom.

Philosophia took a further step in its development as an archangel when Steiner published *Christianity as a Mystical Fact* in 1902.[2] The end of the Kali Yuga in 1899 gave way to the birth of the Age of Light. The prohibitions against revealing spiritual knowledge ceased, and Steiner began lecturing on the stages of initiation as they could be found in the various religions of the world. With the formation of the German section of the Theosophical Society in 1902, he found an audience open to the idea of the unity of all religions. He could begin to combat the prejudice of some Eastern religious leaders that Jesus was a minor prophet and not comparable to the great attainments of Gautama Buddha and other bodhisattvas. Just as Aristotle had brought the phenomena of nature into the realm of the scientific method and the laws of logic, so at the beginning of the twentieth century Steiner brought his audience worlds of soul and spirit from the branch of knowledge that he called spiritual science. He also suggested that people should address the spiritual being inspiring such knowledge with the name of Anthroposophia.

In 1904, Steiner presented his insights into the worlds of soul and spirit in a more thoroughgoing fashion in his third basic book, *Theosophy*. In chapter one he explored the spiritual and soul members of man's inner being, in chapter two he explained the formation of destiny during the reincarnation of the human spirit or ego, and in chapter three he described the experiences of the human spirit in the different regions of the astral and heavenly worlds before its return to the earthly plane of existence. The final chapter focused on a specific series of meditations that are key to the successful entrance of the human being into the spiritual world through initiation.[3] Gautama Buddha offered the eightfold path to mankind in the fourth of his four noble truths. Rudolf Steiner gave a similar path to mankind more than two millennia later. The sixfold path was especially suited for the preparation of the heart chakra for enlightenment, whereas Gautama's meditation prepared the throat chakra. Clearly, both are necessary for initiation, though in the modern age of freedom, Steiner believed that a balancing of the three souls forces of thinking, feeling, and willing would be of primary importance to avoid the aberrations of the bipolar disorders that are prevalent in the present day.

Steiner's fourth basic book was written in what he would come to identify as the first stage of the development of the Anthroposophical Movement from

1902 to 1909. *Knowledge of the Higher Worlds* focused on the development of the astral organs of the human soul (also called the lotus flowers or chakras) in the first half of the book and then, in the second half, on their imprinting on the human etheric body or life body.[4] Steiner clarified why the sixfold path plays such a central role in balancing the seven chakras. He also emphasized that the whole series of six meditations should not require the student to spend more than ten to fifteen minutes a day on them. The tendency in modern times for active people to have no time for meditation and for meditants to spend inordinate amounts of time on their meditative exercises had to be overcome. Steiner believed that one of the missions of Gautama after his rise to Buddhahood involved his activity in the realm of the archetypes of minerals— i.e., in the Mars sphere of lower Devachan—to allow active people to carve out a brief ten minutes at the same time each day so that the spiritual world could enter their lives in a helpful way.

The close of the first stage of the Anthroposophical Movement in 1909 was marked by the publication of *Occult Science: An Outline*. Steiner attempted the strange feat of coining a modern spiritually scientific terminology out of the materialistic natural science of his time. In chapter four of *Occult Science*, Steiner recast the vision that he had had of the Akashic Record and that he had published as *Cosmic Memory* into a picture of the evolution of the seven planets using the spiritualized concepts of Darwinian evolution. *Occult Science* was a synthesis of Western concepts and the Eastern nomenclature of the third and fourth basic books.[5] The four streams of mystery wisdom that find themselves represented in the first five basic books show a resolute effort by Steiner to present Anthroposophy—i.e., the sun archangel that Philosophia had become—in the languages of all four mystery streams.[6] Then Steiner could reach all people, and Anthroposophia could become active in their thought life. His readers could be lifted out of themselves and awakened to the truth of active thinking as it transformed an outline into an imagination.

The sixth basic book was also a book written for the general public and contained within it a complete path of initiation into the higher worlds. In 1914, toward the end of the second stage of the Anthroposophical Movement's development, Rudolf Steiner published *Riddles of Philosophy*. It characterized the history of philosophy from the time of the pre-Socratic thinkers in ancient Greece down to the end of the nineteenth century in Europe. Greek philosophy attained a certain height with Aristotle. The Christian Era began slowly, but with the advent of Scotus Erigena, philosophy developed further and reached another high point with the theology of Aquinas in the time of Scholasticism. The modern age of freedom began with a thunderclap like that of Luther nailing the *Ninety-five Theses* to a church door. The Protestant revelation that the conscience is the voice of God within the human soul—the spirit guide of the true self—found its counterpart in the philosophy of Descartes in his "Cogito ergo sum": the I becomes aware of itself as an "ego" through its activity in forming thoughts.[7] Modern philosophy achieved a similar height to that of Aristotle in Athens and Aquinas in Paris with the logical idealism of Hegel in Germany. Steiner's own contribution to that effort—his first basic book, written in 1894—is not recognized as important, but as Steiner himself suggested, it might prove to be his most lasting achievement.

Steiner completed his final basic book, *The Course of My Life*, on his deathbed in 1925. He pointed out that his autobiography showed the soul and spiritual development of an individual ego, and not the overshadowing by a bodhisattva of one of his pupils. Even before his death, members of the Anthroposophical Society were conjecturing about which human bodhisattva Steiner might have been. Since Steiner had informed some members of the truth of his earlier incarnations and a century has passed since his death, several books have appeared that document in Steiner's earlier lives in detail.[8] Steiner offered a reason for writing his autobiography. He maintained that a human being who appeared publicly as an initiate by writing a basic book or lecturing about esoteric matters, etc., must reveal his path of development in an autobiography so that people who are interested in his ideas can make a fully informed decision about whether to take them up. Gandhi's autobiography clearly was written for a reason similar to that of Steiner.

The first stage of the development of the Anthroposophical Movement included Steiner's publication of four of the seven basic books. The first basic book, *The Philosophy of Freedom*, was written before this stage. It helped to clarify the change that occurred in philosophy with the birth of Anthroposophia. While philosophy tends to be read intellectually, the basic books of anthroposophy need to be viewed as paths to the truth. The first step is to study anthroposophy and then to experience its truth or falsity in one's own life. Only a willingness to live by the truth as revealed in one's own life experiences can lead to soul development in a proper way. The goal of study is not knowledge, but wisdom and truth. The next step is meditation, and the slow, gradual attempt to build up one's character through the attainment of certain virtues. Steiner's past lives, especially those of Aristotle and Aquinas, show why he was so eminently qualified to take on the task of assisting the transformations of philosophy and theology into anthroposophy. The other reason that the mission of founding Anthroposophy was so vital to Steiner can be surmised by considering the discussion of the role of Thomas Paine in the Revolutionary War.[9]

Paine's earlier incarnation as Caesar Augustus made him the founder of the Roman Empire and of the idea of kingship. Paine was responsible for the misuse of this idea in the age of freedom, and he thus played an active role in restoring the rights of man. Aristotle's philosophy had served the high purpose of bringing logic and reason into human society, but in the modern age its tendency to intellectualism had to be overcome. Only a renewal of the idea of reincarnation could enable modern people to discover the truth of their character and of their destiny and overcome the materialism of the natural science that has arisen from Aristotelianism.

Just as philosophy had to go through a transition period at the beginning of the new sun regency in 1879, so did the spirit of neoclassicism. From its beginning in ancient Greece as the god Apollo, to its activity in early Christian times as Catholicism, to its transformation at the beginning of the modern age into the Renaissance, this spirit of Neoclassicism helped inspire the Greek tragedians, the tragedies of Shakespeare, and, at the beginning of the sun regency, the modern tragedies of Henrik Ibsen—especially his play "An Enemy of the People" in 1879. Other extraordinary dramatists arose with the end of the Kali Yuga (the Age of Darkness) and the birth of the Age of Light in 1899. In Russia, the plays of Anton Chekhov continued the tradition begun by Dostoyevsky and Tolstoy. "The Seagull," "The Cherry Orchard," and other plays brought the soul trials of modern human beings to the stage. Not the lesser mysteries of the fire and water trials presented to ancient Greeks, but a modern form of the air trial appropriate for the age of freedom inspired the Russian audiences. George Bernard Shaw accomplished a similar deed for English audiences, especially with "Heartbreak House."

Neoclassicism extended the scope of its influence on literature and drama to the fine arts as well. The architectural marvel of the Parthenon and glory of Athena's statue held within it found its counterpart in the Italian Renaissance with Michelangelo's dome for St. Peter's Cathedral and his statue of David and his "Pieta." With the advent of the archangel of the sun's regency, the City Beautiful Movement began to coalesce in Chicago for the World's Fair of 1893. The White City and the statue of "The Republic" that these architects and sculptors created gave promise of what they would achieve a decade later in Washington, D.C. In the new Age of Light, they took on the Freemasonic task of finding a proper form for a pillar of the Temple of Liberty. Their achievement, the Lincoln Memorial, opened to the public in 1922. Henry Bacon's vision, inspired by the Parthenon itself, contained within it a statue of Lincoln by America's foremost sculptor, Daniel Chester French.

In the second stage of the development of the Anthroposophical Movement from 1909 to 1916, Rudolf

Steiner devoted himself to working with this Apollonian spirit of neoclassicism. Between 1910 and 1913 he wrote, directed, and produced a new Mystery Drama each year. He even created a new artistic form called eurythmy, which he taught to others and incorporated in his dramas. The onset of World War I—the guns of August—prevented the production of a fifth play, but Steiner gave a lecture cycle in 1914 that helped clarify the deeper meanings that abound for students of *The Portal of Initiation* and the three other plays. His lectures on "Human and Cosmic Thought" showed the circle of twelve characters that appeared in each of the plays, their virtues and weaknesses and their collaborators and nemeses.[10]

The second stage saw a shift in Steiner's attention from the Mystery Dramas to creating a building in which to house their performance. His focus on architectural forms and a sculpture was made possible by an international collection of artists and would-be-colleagues who spent their days during the war building and crafting the singularly remarkable and beautiful first Goetheanum. As usual, Steiner felt it necessary to create new kinds of painting, of stained-glass, and of architectural forms. He took personal responsibility for sculpting "The Representative of Man," the centerpiece of the double-domed structure uniting the East and the West. Neither did Steiner ignore the importance of assisting Philosophia's metamorphosis into Anthroposophia during this second stage by publishing *The Riddles of Philosophy* in 1914.

World War I caused Steiner to cease productions of the Mystery Dramas and to focus on building the Goetheanum in Dornach, Switzerland, which was a neutral country. Steiner understood the basic cause of the war: that the world economy had emerged from the interweaving of the production of goods and the distribution of goods among the many nations in the world. The need to understand economic concepts properly was barely recognized, and problems arising in the economic sphere were seen through the professorial lens that belonged to national economists. For example, many professors of economics thought that the war would be over quickly, a year at most. Steiner believed that these adherents of the ideas of Adam Smith could not grasp that the world economy would drag all countries into the conflict. The members of the Western secret societies—for example Skull and Bones at Yale and The Group at Oxford—accelerated the process, as Steiner exhaustively documented in *The Karma of Untruthfulness*, a group of twenty-five lectures given in 1916 and early 1917.

A more sinister part of the plan of the Western secret societies involved what they called the socialist experiment. Its purpose was to present a false antithesis to the economic system of capitalism. The

Western secret societies wanted people to think that the Communism of Lenin and the purges of Stalin—rather than Socialism—were the antithesis of capitalism. They wanted to hide how a synthesis of capitalism and socialism could lead to an insight into how to manage capitalism in a functioning world economy and then how to unite it with the world soul in the sphere of human rights so that governments could truly serve the people. The October Revolution was a cul-de-sac of history that lasted for 72 years, as Steiner correctly predicted. Germany sent Lenin's train to St. Petersburg, the U.S. fleet prevented the czar's escape, and England, with the help of Pershing's U.S. Expeditionary Force, won the war more than four years after it had begun. What Steiner tried to do to counter the successes of the Western secret societies was take the ideas in his book *The Threefold Society*, lecture on them, and educate people so that they could have a picture of a world economy that did not exploit, but healed.

The Western secret societies also viewed World War I as an opportunity to prepare for the second phase of the plan of King James I of Great Britain. Their goal was to create a cultural counterpart to the Roman Catholicism in Europe during the Middle Ages and thereby attain hegemony over the world. They wanted to misuse the mechanical genius native to the Anglo-Saxon people and develop a commercial, computerized, materialistic culture which is now usually called Americanism. It would replace the arts and literature of Idealism with sports, entertainment, and a lifestyle dependent on a highly advanced technology using sub-earthly forces. These secret societies saw the greatest threat to their plan in the achievements of German culture. Rudolf Steiner was deemed the Number One enemy of the Third Reich by the Nazi Party. When the Goetheanum was burned to the ground on December 31, 1922, the body of the man who set the blaze and died in the conflagration was identified as that of a Nazi. While World War I may have been inevitable, as Steiner believed, the complete destruction of Germany's economy due to the terms of the Treaty of Versailles was not. Rather the secret societies worked actively to prevent any possible renewal of Idealism or Anthroposophy.

The guardian and protector of the Grail stream and Rosicrucianism in the Middle Ages was Michael, whom Steiner called the archangel of esoteric Christianity. This archangel of the sun had enabled Parzival and Christian Rosenkreutz to lay the first two foundation stones of the New Jerusalem as truly free deeds, mankind's own contribution to his future heavenly home. It is Michael who protects the sphere of freedom so that human thinking, when it becomes self-aware and active, remains free of all other influences, good or bad. Human beings are indeed special, and it is their gifts of love, given in freedom, that will shape the future. Michael was also active at the beginning of the sun regency in 1879 with the founding of the Theosophical Society by Madame Blavatsky. Rudolf Steiner joined this esoteric society in 1902, after the beginning of the Age of Light. Two years later the leader of the Theosophical Society, Annie Besant, gave Steiner permission to conduct lessons in its Esoteric School.[11] In 1904, Steiner was also invited to lead a Freemasonic lodge. He accepted and gave lectures to its members under the belief that the birth of the Age of Light meant that the need for secrecy had passed and that the truths of the spirit world should be available to all earnest seekers.

Michael led the third stage of the development of the Anthroposophical Movement from 1916 to 1923. In a similar way, Anthroposophia had led the first stage and Apollo (through Neoclassicism) had led the second. Steiner's attempt to bring the idea of the threefold society to the general public in 1918 and 1919 was not met favorably enough to have any realistic hope of success. He took up other social initiatives instead. He began with the founding of the first Waldorf School in 1919. A new form of education emerged. It was based on the divine nature of the ego incarnating in the young child, the four temperaments, the seven-year cycle of childhood in the elementary school years, and the cycle of adolescence in high school and college. In

1920, Steiner gave a course on medicine to doctors.[12] In the following year, Ita Wegman opened a clinic for Anthroposophical medicine and then worked with Steiner in writing *Fundamentals of Therapy*.[13] What became the social initiative of Biodynamic agriculture started in 1922 in a laboratory run by Guenther Wachsmuth and Ehrenfried Pfeiffer. Two years later Steiner's suggestions for biodynamic preparations could be applied and used in practical ways on a working farm.[14]

The burning of the Goetheanum in winter of 1922-23 led Steiner to the decision to build a second one. This structure would not be made of wood and stained glass and Norwegian slate, but it would be a modern building made of steel and concrete. Steiner drew the architectural design and explained to his co-workers how to develop further the new artistic impulses that the spirit of Apollo/neoclassicism had brought alive in the first Goetheanum. Steiner made a second decision as well. On the first anniversary of the Goetheanum's burning, he planned to re-found the Anthroposophical Society during what he called the Christmas Conference. The Anthroposophical Society had swelled to twelve thousand members, all of whom had a membership card personally signed by Steiner. To make his intent even more clear, Steiner called the document that brought about the re-founding of the Anthroposophical Society the Foundation Stone meditation. Steiner hoped to open the third gate to the

New Jerusalem with a free deed like those of Parzival and Rosenkreutz. Not an epic like *Parzival* or a vision like *The Alchymical Wedding of Christian Rosenkreutz*, but a meditation in four parts was offered up to Michael to accept or reject as a gateway—the third gate—to the Grail Castle in the land of Providence, the home of the bodhisattvas where the Spirits of Truth interweave to form the Grail Cup wherein dwells the Mystic Lamb. In January of 1924 Steiner informed the leaders of the new Anthroposophical Society that Michael had indeed approved of his free deed. Next Steiner began giving lectures to the members of the First Class of the School for Spiritual Science. These lectures included nineteen mantras which elucidate the pathway to our true home in important detail. After the passage of nearly a century, these nineteen mantras and the pathway itself have entered the public domain and are available to anyone who is interested.

CHAPTER SEVEN NOTES

[1] A full discussion of the stages of the knowledge of freedom and of the reality of freedom is given in Spaulding, *The Basic Books of Rudolf Steiner* and on the two charts on pp. 52 and 58 in the same book.

[2] See the summary of Steiner's *Christianity as a Mystical Fact* in *The Basic Books of Rudolf Steiner*, pp. 40-44.

[3] See also the charts on pp. 10, 11, and 13 in *The Basic Books of Rudolf Steiner.*

---

[4] See charts on pp. 24-25 of *The Basic Books of Rudolf Steiner.*

[5] See chart on p.34 of *The Basic Books of Rudolf Steiner.*

[6] See p. 58 of the same.

[7] See Rudolf Grosse, *The Living Being of Anthroposophia*, pp. 55-56.

[8] See Bockholt's *Rudolf Steiner's Mission and Ita Wegman*

[9] See Chapter 6 of this book, "The Age of Freedom."

[10] See chart on p.14 in *Parzival Mystery Stream in the Twentieth Century.*

[11] See Steiner's lectures to the Esoteric School in the *Collected* Works, CW 264-266.

[12] See Steiner, CW 312.

[13] See Steiner, CW 27.

[14] See *The Basic Books of Rudolf Steiner*, pp.96-104.

Chapter 8:
the Beast of the Apocalypse

A DOLF HITLER BECAME PRESIDENT OF THE National Socialist German Workers Party in July 1921. He gathered around him many of the future leaders of the Nazi Party. His power was essentially absolute. By 1922 Hitler declared Rudolf Steiner to be the Number One enemy of the Third Reich and even ordered an assassination attempt be made on his life. When the attempt failed, Steiner returned to Dornach, Switzerland, and ceased giving public lectures on the threefold society and holding rallies to support it. By the end of 1922, Hitler succeeded in getting rid of Steiner's greatest artistic achievement by burning the Goetheanum to the ground. If Hitler had been able to assassinate Steiner, the opening of the third gate of the New Jerusalem would not have occurred in January 1924.

A pupil of Rudolf Steiner, Walter Johannes Stein, became a founding teacher of the first Waldorf School in 1919. In 1922, Steiner chose him to teach *Parzival* to a class of juniors and answered his many questions on Wolfram's masterpiece. By 1928, Stein was ready to publish his research in a commentary on *Parzival* titled *The Ninth Century and the Holy Grail*. His greatest insight was in identifying the three pillars of *Parzival*.[1] He also did extensive research on Klingsor, Parzival's opponent and lord of the Castle of Wonders, the evil counterpart of the Grail Castle. Stein found the historical counterpart of Klingsor in the figure of Landulf II of Capua, a practitioner of black magic. Klingsor's attacks on Sir Gawain were meant to distract Parzival and prevent him from laying the first foundation stone and opening the first gate of the home of the Grail in the world of Providence—the Grail Castle.

Johannes Tautz, the leader of the Pedagogical Section, who came to Spring Valley, New York, in 1982 to found the pedagogical section of the School for Spiritual Science in America, wrote a biography, *W. J. Stein*, in 1993. He confirmed the major role that Rudolf Steiner had played in Stein's life as his spirit guide. He also examined Stein's insights into his own past earthly lives, especially his incarnation as Trevrizent, the brother of Anfortas, who was the lord of the Grail Castle. Trevrizent became the spiritual adviser to Parzival, who in 869 became the new leader of the Grail knights. Stein explained the role that Trevrizent had played in his commentary on *Parzival*, published in 1928. Trevrizent's mission was to make up for the weakness of his brother by becoming a hermit and leading a life of piety to atone for the latter's worldliness. Tautz indicated that this quality of Trevrizent was basic to his character and had reappeared in his life as Walter Stein. Stein again played the role of an agent of balance, though not with the reincarnated Anfortas, but with Rudolf Steiner himself. Stein became a lecturer par excellence, a fiery orator whom Steiner kept in reserve and brought out to speak only on the most important occasions. Stein lectured on the idea of the threefold society and how its implementation could lead to freedom in the cultural sphere, equality in the sociology-political system, and brotherhood in the economic realm. Steiner had told Stein in 1923 that Gandhi was the greatest truth-speaker alive and that he should emulate him. When Stein did meet Gandhi, he gave him a copy of Steiner's *Threefold Society*. Stein also worked with Dunlop in 1932 on a large-scale plan, the World Economic Union, for which Stein gave powerful lectures. Dunlop's unfortunate death prevented the spread of these basic economic concepts and allowed the false economic ideas of the present day to remain unchallenged.

Hitler was elected to the office of chancellor in 1933. By the following year, when he adopted the title of "Führer," the takeover of the German government was fully accomplished. A thirteen-year dictatorship began its attack on German culture. The goal of the Asura that possessed Hitler, especially in his speeches,

was to smother German culture. Writers like Mann
and Hesse and theologians like Tillich fled the country. University professors and clergymen were
investigated, and very few spoke out. The German
Christian Movement came to include most of the Protestant denominations and their churches, and it
granted them protection from the persecution of
Nazism. Bonhoeffer was the lone minister who spoke
out and protested Hitler's evil, while the two leaders of
the White Rose, a political group active in German
universities, were the lone political opponents to challenge the Nazis. All three protesters were imprisoned
in concentration camps and executed.

A book by Trevor Ravenscroft in 1973, *The Spear
of Destiny*, clarified Hitler's real purpose—the practice
of the ABCs of black magic. While inaccurate in many
details, Ravenscroft's book is at least an attempt to
uncover the real danger of Nazism.[2] Rudolf Steiner
gave a lecture cycle on *The Apocalypse of St. John* in
Nuremberg in 1908. In it, Steiner explained that the
real threat to mankind was not the one-sided materialism of the Ahrimanic powers or the equally
one-sided spiritualism of the Luciferic beings that
opposed earthly life, but the black magic emanating
from the leader of the third hierarchy of evil, Sorath—
the two-horned beast of the Apocalypse. Before
Steiner's death in 1925, he told Rittlemeyer, the leader
of the Christian Community of churches that Steiner

himself had helped to found, that Sorath would begin to work in the earthly realm around the year 1933. Sorath's emissaries would no longer be his principle means of destroying that cosmos of love that the twelve divine Spirits of Truth were trying to build in the world of Providence. The appearance of Sorath on the earthly plane required a human being to be especially prepared so that Sorath could possess him corporeally, a kind of demonic counterpart to the Christ spirit entering Jesus's earthly body at the time of the Baptism in 30 A.D. Those who have heard Hitler speak on radio broadcasts or on televised recordings generally notice how power and magnetism seem to flow from him and entrance the crowd. Many even refer to Hitler's speeches as "possessed," though few can grasp the idea that such possession is itself a form of black magic.

The Nazi form of black magic begins with its central symbol, the swastika. The ancient form of a right-facing swastika (with arms bending forward[3]) is a symbolic picture of the root chakra, the seventh of the astral organs of man's soul body and the first to be activated in the Indian (or Eastern) form of initiation into the higher spiritual worlds. The Nazi swastika also has its arms bending to the right, but is tilted at a forty-five degree angle. Very few members knew of the magic of Sorath when, in the torchlight parades of the Nazi Party, they held their torches and formed up into the shape of the Nazi swastika, which then began to rotate in a counter-clockwise direction as they marched, signifying that the initiation of Nazism begins by making the root chakra revolve in the opposite direction of its normal clockwise rotation. Sorath's power over the souls of those who mindlessly surrendered to him, however, was all the greater. The human spirit thusly perverted would not rise into the higher spheres of the hierarchy of angels, but be cast downwards into sub-earthly and demonic regions.

Another aspect of the Nazi form of black magic was its reliance on the "Big Lie." Hitler never tired of blaming the Jews for Germany's defeat in World War I, especially repeating the idea of Jews stabbing the Aryan race in the back. Sorath doesn't just enjoy the mindlessness of his followers, he demands it of them by requiring them to accept as true what is in fact a bald lie. Germany's defeat in World War I came at the hands of the Western secret societies in England and America, not Jewish bankers. These secret societies feared that German culture would lead to freedom and therefore pose a danger to the spread of the kind of magic that they intended to use selfishly rather than for the good of all of mankind. The challenge that the big lie and the black magic of Nazism posed to the churches and educational institutions of Germany also applied to other cultural groups, especially to the Anthroposophical Society. The Society knew as well as anyone what Nazism had in store for those who opposed them. More than a decade before Hitler's rise to power, the Anthroposophical Society experienced an attempted assassination of its leader and the burning of its headquarters to the ground. After Steiner's death, Stein, the Society's most dynamic lecturer continued to speak about the threefold society until finally fleeing to England in 1933. By 1935, the leadership group of the Society actually split over the question of Hitler, and three of the leaders of the Society expelled two other leaders along with Walter Stein and Willem Zeylmans van Emmichoven, who felt duty-bound to stand against the fear and terror that black magic tried to instill in its opponents. With the growth of the Hitler Youth camps, the Waldorf School movement in Germany also shut down with hardly a whimper.

After Hitler completed his takeover of the government in Germany and established a fascist dictatorship, he turned his sights on the German military and began to carry out the foreign policy objectives that he had written about in his autobiography, *Mein Kampf.* He withdrew from the League of Nations, introduced conscription, remilitarized the Rhineland, established the Rome-Berlin axis, occupied Austria, and invaded Poland. When Hitler launched his invasion of the U.S.S.R. on June 22, 1941, he began to place more importance on the SS divisions that were directly responsible to him. Using the Gestapo (the secret police) to expand the concentration camps, to create extermination camps like Auschwitz, and to form mobile extermination squads, Hitler prepared what he referred to as the "final solution" to the Jewish problem. On the Eastern battlefront of the war, Stalin's Commissar-infested Soviet army and Hitler's Gestapo-infested Nazi army between them claimed the lives of over fifteen million soldiers. Since neither side cared much about civilian casualties, another ten million non-soldiers lost their lives as well. On his deathbed in 1952, Stalin made plans for a million Communists to perish in a purge, but he died before he could bring the plan to fruition.

According to Steiner's explanation of the significance of the year 1933, which he explained to Rittelmeyer, World War II was a distraction. The real importance of 1933 was that it would be the beginning of Christ's reappearance on the earthly plane in a spiritual form like that which St. Paul had experienced on his journey to Damascus. Steiner believed that 1933 would mark the advent of the Second Coming and the call of Christ to inspire human beings to prepare to enter the world of mankind's future, the realm of Nirvana. The forces of Sorath decided instead to occupy mankind with something else: a world war, laced with the fervor of nationalism and blind favoritism of one's own country over the enemy's. World War II offered the corrupt and decadent Western secret societies, as well as their Bolshevik allies, a chance to evaluate how far the cultivation of black magicians had advanced.

Hitler's final solution can be seen as a later stage of the Roman gladiators in their practice of the ABCs of black magic. In their future incarnations the gladiators served as soldiers of the Crusades, as priests of the Inquisition, as the crews of the slave ships, and as the slave-tamers on the plantations. As members of the Gestapo, they had learned to enjoy the pain that they caused when torturing people and how to murder someone to gain even more power. The Nuremberg Trials that followed the Allied victory did acknowledge the six million victims of the Nazi concentration camps, but they effectively whitewashed the black magic at its core. More importantly, they justified the partition of Germany and achieved their goal of eliminating German culture as a danger to the hegemony of Americanism in the coming century. The East Germans were offered the Socialist Man as a hero to emulate in an Orwellian world of Big Brother surveillance, while the West Germans succumbed to a world of sex, drugs, and rock 'n' roll, and became increasingly commercial, materialistic, and technology-bound. With the collapse of Bolshevism in 1989, the partition of Germany also ended, but unified Germany still lacked any new cultural impulses and wallowed in the wasteland of Americanism.

The possibility that Adolf Hitler may have been the reincarnation of Klingsor—or the historical personage of Landulf II of Capua, according to Stein's research—is corroborated by Wolfram's characterization of Klingsor as a black magician. Klingsor was unsuccessful in his attempt to divert Parzival from his mission to become the Lord of the Grail and to open the first gate to the Grail Castle. Likewise, Hitler failed in his attempt to assassinate Rudolf Steiner and prevent him from laying the foundation stone for the third gate of the New Jerusalem. Hitler did succeed, however, in burning down the Goetheanum, the first mystery center built so that the general public could enter it and experience its artistic beauty and holy truth. Its loss was incalculable. Its windows and columns, its double-domed roof and auditorium, could have turned many visitors to a path of the spirit and dealt Sorath a mighty blow.

During the time of Hitler's rise to power with Nazism, an American played a similar role, though in a much more hidden and behind-the-scenes kind of way. In 1917, J. Edgar Hoover joined the organization in the Justice Department that would become the Federal Bureau of Investigation. His first task was to make a list of Germans living in America who should be detained without the right to *habeas corpus*. By 1921, he became its temporary director, and in 1924 the permanent one. His tenure lasted half a century. Hoover joined a Freemasonic Lodge in 1920 and rose to its pinnacle of power by becoming a Mason of the thirty-third degree.

Hoover's first major operation as America's head of law enforcement was called by historians "The Red Scare." The FBI attacks on the growing labor movement involved discrediting labor leaders by branding them as Bolsheviks. Many had to flee the country or go underground to avoid imprisonment or worse. Hoover began the practice of having his agents make a list of the most powerful—and therefore most dangerous—speakers, which he called the Index. He also conducted illegal surveillance and hired agents provocateurs to infiltrate unions and tarnish their names. He essentially ignored the existence of organized crime. When the public outcry against the Mafia became impossible to ignore, he formed a task force under the leadership of Eliot Ness. The success of the Untouchables became a national sensation, but Hoover resorted to smearing Ness and downplaying the danger posed by the mob. Instead, he continued building out his files of hundreds of thousands of American "subversives", including Felix Frankfurter—an Associate Justice of the Supreme Court and an Austrian-American Jew—which gives some indication of the depths of his racism. The fact that Hoover hired no women agents during this first stage of his time as FBI director suggests the opinion that he held of women.

The second stage of Hoover's time as director began in the middle of the 1950s, when he assembled the Counterintelligence Program (COINTELPRO for short) and required it to be implemented in all FBI branch offices. The threat of the Civil Rights movement, from Hoover's viewpoint, justified COINTELPRO, and he continued to revise it and reissue it as increasingly drastic measures to halt the spread of Civil Rights protests seemed, to him, to be necessary. The March on Washington in 1963 quickly gave way to the assassination of Present Kennedy three months later. Hoover took full charge of the investigation into JFK's murder. When his findings met with public disbelief and anger, the Warren Commission was formed to give the whitewash a proper veneer.

By the middle of the 1960s, even more stringent measures were taken to ensure that the black communities in America would not become fertile ground for the Civil Rights movement and the emerging human rights movement. As Britain had done in the 1830s in China, large quantities of opium were dumped into the areas that seemed rebellious. The United States government targeted black communities in large urban areas as havens for the drug trade. A weak military and an inability to carry out surveillance were not the reasons this country was unable to stop drug trafficking. On the contrary, the Federal government helped to fund black gangs like the Blackstone Rangers and Devil's Disciples in Chicago, who not only received large grants but were completely infiltrated by FBI informants and agents provocateurs.

The CIA played a similar role internationally. It insured a steady supply of this poison, which Western secret societies—like Hoover's own lodge—planned to use to suppress the freedom movements. The region in southeast Asia most famous for supplying opium was even named the golden triangle.

The FBI also resorted to the tactic of targeted assassinations. Malcom X's assassination became the subject of the 2020, six-part documentary "Who Killed Malcolm?" Its conclusion was that though the FBI didn't carry it out, the agency was responsible for arranging it. Even Malcolm's personal bodyguard was a New York police officer working undercover. The King family, as well, refused to accept James Earl Ray's guilt in the assassination of Dr. King, and time has confirmed their belief that he was just a fall guy. The murder that led to the truth about these assassinations being finally told occurred the following year on December 4, 1969. In Chicago, the police told the press the story of a gun battle with the Black Panthers when they executed an after-midnight raid searching for illegal weapons, but the evidence of the shell casings and bullet holes at the scene showed that the police fired about 100 shots and the Panthers none. The survivors and the families of Fred Hampton and Mark Clark, both murdered in the raid, ended up suing the Cook County State's Attorney Edward Hanrahan and the FBI. The case was not settled until

1983 when the plaintiffs were awarded almost two million dollars in damages. During the case, which became a series of trials, the existence of Hoover's plan was entered as evidence. An anti-war group raided an FBI branch office in 1971, discovered a copy of COIN-TELPRO, and began releasing its contents. Jeffrey Haas, a lawyer for the Hampton family, published a book showing in detail how the FBI and the Chicago Police murdered Fred Hampton.[4] In 1969, J. Edgar Hoover labeled the Black Panther Party the most dangerous group in America. Twenty-nine Panthers were murdered in that year, including Fred Hampton.

One of the most remarkable passages in Hoover's COINTELPRO is his articulation of the goals of his program. He especially wanted to prevent the rise of a Black Messiah, even stating that Malcolm X might have been such a leader and that Dr. King aspired to the position. Hoover called for such threats to be "neutralized" and their organizations to be discredited. The detailed plans that the FBI exchanged with the Chicago police assigned to Hanrahan's office included information received from William O'Neal, who was the Panther's chief of security and an FBI informant. His handler even wrote a personal letter to Director Hoover requesting a sizable bonus for O'Neal since his information proved so valuable to the raid.

Some further insight into Hoover's extraordinary cruelty, cunning, and fear-inspiring reign can be gained by turning our gaze from the near-past to his possible past lives. The possibility that Hoover was the reincarnation of the governmental leader who tried to kill the Messiah of Biblical times—Herod the Great—might help to illuminate his strange idea of neutralizing and murdering a great savior of the Black people in the twentieth century. In the Sanhedrin, Herod had the equivalent of the Freemasonic Lodge of which Hoover became the leader. For a group of rabbinical scholars and wise men to reveal where the Messiah was destined to be born to a Roman governor makes little sense, unless they too had become corrupted and desired to advance the reign of Sorath and his black magic. Perhaps their fear of the King of Judea, whom historians say was suffering from mental decay, could be given as an explanation. Hoover provoked a similar widespread fear within governmental circles. Even Presidents were said to fear him, though John Kennedy may not have. Herod's other weaknesses are also echoed in the life of Hoover. His cruelty, exhibited in the slaughter of the innocents, echoes in the drumbeat of assassinations carried out under his watch, and Herod's extreme jealousy of his many wives in Hoover's envy of Ness and any agent other than himself who was praised for success.

In the Presidential campaign of 2016, a Republican candidate arose who—like Hitler—mesmerized his followers with speeches that spewed hatred and vitriol.

Donald Trump began his campaign by attacking Latinos and promising that he would build a wall to keep Latino immigrants out, but that Mexico would pay for it. After he won the election, he continued to hold campaign-like rallies and bask in his adoring crowds. He held up other groups as scapegoats. When the Covid-19 pandemic hit the shores of America, President Trump initiated an ineffective and unwarranted ban on Muslim immigration. When the virus caused still more deaths and slowed the economy, he blamed the Chinese. Since he had so many followers on social media and so many supporters in right-wing extremist groups who took his words as a call to arms, hate crimes against Muslims and Asians increased dramatically. When police murders of black men continued to rise and protests led by Black Lives Matter organizers were covered by national news outlets, President Trump actually formed a national police force that he sent to break up their protests, most famously in Seattle. The FBI was also active in its own way, sending agents provocateurs into and around the protests to loot stores and cause riots that could be blamed on the Black Lives Matter movement.

The virulence of Trump's support among right-wing militia groups, the Ku Klux Klan, Neo-Nazis, and others struck fear into the Republican Party. Trump's own hatred for anyone who dared to challenge him led to blistering personal attacks on his opponents, while in the background loomed the terrorist threats of the followers of Trump who called him the "god emperor" and swore fealty to him as if in remembrance of their Führer. Trump chose to stoke the fires of white supremacy and American nationalism with his slogan, "Make America Great Again" (MAGA). He opposed international groups, withdrew from the Paris Climate Accords and World Health Organization, and threatened to disrupt or leave the United Nations and NATO. Trump's foreign policy seemed to consist of his friendships with dictators, like those in North Korea and Turkey. His relationship with Vladimir Putin seems to reflect the spiritual influence of Sorath on both Hitler and Stalin almost a century ago. Trump is not a master of black magic like Hitler was, but he is an apparent and willing vessel of Sorath, nonetheless.

Trump's most characteristic quality seems to be his pretense of divinity. On the day he announced his first candidacy for office—after the famous ride down the escalator at Trump Tower on June 16, 2015—a message appeared on the Internet chat board 4chan proclaiming the arrival of the God Emperor. That December a five-minute video was posted to YouTube entitled "Donald Trump Emperor of Mankind," celebrating the appearance of the "god emperor." In March 2016, Milo Yiannopoulous—British journalist, noted white supremacist, and creator of the Twitter feed @Nero—clarified in an interview that when he used the term "Daddy" he was referring to Donald, "the god emperor and his incoming Trumpen-reich."[5] His cabinet ministers are his underlings, his fellow Republican Party members are his servants, and they both must praise him. No lie is too outlandish when praising the man responsible for a half of a million deaths from the pandemic by the time he left office. The god-emperor of Rome was one of the evil emperors, Caligula, whose own pretense of divinity rivaled that of Trump's. Near the end of his reign, Caligula had ordered that a stature of himself be placed in the Temple of Solomon—at the point of the sword if necessary—but the sacrilegious act was opposed through mass non-violent protests by tens of thousands of Jewish peasants.[6] After Trump left office in 2021, an artist made a golden statue of the man with orange hair, which debuted the weekend that Trump addressed the Conservative Political Action Committee (CPAC) in his first public speech after leaving office. It has showed up at many of Trump's rallies since then.

Trump shared other qualities with Caligula. Caligula, for example, was known for his cruelty to his opponents, especially evident in his re-instatement of bloody and chaotic treason trials in 39 A.D. and his brutal exile or execution of any he suspected of disloyalty, even those closest to him. Trump's own cruelty extended from vilifying his opponents to keeping migrant children in cages at the U.S. border facilities. Caligula was rumored to have committed incest with

his sister, Drusilla, and he, after her death, had the gall
to have her deified and her head put on a Roman coin.
Trump's Access Hollywood tape similarly revealed
how completely perverse his idea of love really was.
Caligula was also known for his extravagance. Like the
real estate developer, the emperor was a builder and a
spendthrift, one who made enormous investments in
developing new Roman infrastructure and thereby
draining the imperial treasury that his predecessor,
Tiberius, had amassed. Trump, in his own right, raised
over a billion dollars for his reelection campaign in
2020 and wasted it away, running out of money in the
final month and draining huge sums of money through
his inauguration festivities. He later ensured that the
U.S. government would continue a long slide into debt
and deficit by giving himself and other extremely rich
people large tax cuts.

A final aspect of Trump's character that belongs
particularly to black magicians is his ability to tell the
"big lie." Hitler's big lie was how Germany lost World
War I; Trump's was how he lost his re-election. A loyal
follower of Trump is required to believe that Trump
won the 2020 election and that voter fraud robbed him
of a second term. The Republican Party is now the
New Nazi Party, whose purpose is to restrict voting
rights and abortion rights—a strange combination of
preparing for dictatorship and bringing Christians on
board, but very like Nazi Germany. On January 6, 2021,

President Trump finally summoned his mob of adherents to the nation's capital, or as he put it, "It'll be wild!" He then unleashed the Proud Boys to lead the mob and take up arms to invade the U.S. Capitol Building. The leaders of the attack on the Capitol threatened to hang Mike Pence and Nancy Pelosi and even built a gallows in front of the Capitol building. Compared to the first attack on the Temple of Liberty by the British army in 1814 during the Second Revolutionary War—when they burned it to the ground—this take-over was largely symbolic. It did, however, serve the purpose to mobilize the forces of darkness and allow the intelligence-gathering forces to identify those who might protest or resist the rise of Trump.

CHAPTER EIGHT NOTES

[1] See the author's book *The Parzival Mystery Stream in the Twentieth Century.*

[2] Ravenscroft was a student of Walter Stein's, as were Rene Querido and Werner Glas who discussed the faults and errors of *The Spear of Destiny* with me.

[3] Both the right-facing or clock-wise swastika (卐) and the left-facing or counter-clockwise swastika (卍) are found in the art of many ancient cultures around the globe—such as the ancient Indian, Greek, and Celtic peoples—as well as in in the religious sphere, for example in Buddhism and Jainism up to the present day. As a symbol, the Nazi swastika

appropriated and corrupted the clock-wise swastika by tilting it at an angle and reversing its rotation. This paragraph suggests the deeper meaning behind that appropriation.

[4] See Jeffery Haas, *The Assassination of Fred Hampton*.

[5] The Rubin Report, March 25, 2016, interview with Milo Yiannopoulos. See also the summary of the "God Emperor" meme on the "Know Your Meme" web site. For a lengthy research article studying the 'God Emperor' meme and other Trump memes on 4chan in 2019, halfway through Trump's term in office, see Way, "Trump Memes and the Alt-right."

[6] For a detailed account of this incident, see Josephus, *Antiquities*, book 18.261-309.

CHAPTER 9:
THE NEW SPIRIT OF TRUTH

I N JANUARY OF 1924, RUDOLF STEINER TOLD THE leaders of the newly re-formed Anthroposophical Society that Michael had accepted his gift given in freedom—the Christmas Conference of 1923 and the laying of the Foundation Stone meditation in the hearts of the Society's twelve thousand members. The pathway to the Grail Castle of Parzival and the second gate opened by Christian Rosenkreutz in 1459 were followed by the opening of a third gate. Steiner began giving lectures to members who had joined the School for Spiritual Science, the esoteric school at the heart of the new Anthroposophical Society. The pathway of the basic books became the nineteen first class lessons, a specific series of mantras and meditations for the members to take up and practice in order to experience the New Jerusalem and the Mystic Lamb contained in the Grail Cup formed by the interweaving of the Spirits of Truth in their heavenly home in Nirvana, the world of Providence. This third gateway is different than the first two in that it is open to all who earnestly seek it since the class lessons and lectures are in the public domain. Any free person can find them, study them, and decide if he or she would wish to become a student of the leaders of the School of Spiritual Science, Christian Rosenkreutz and Rudolf Steiner. At this point it is important to realize that Michael's approval of Steiner's free deed also signified Rudolf Steiner's ascension into the realm of the human bodhisattvas. Despite not having been initiated in any of his previous lives, Rudolf Steiner became the thirteenth Master of Wisdom and the Harmony of Feelings. He blazed a path that other human beings may follow, since human beings can only themselves emulate a deed that has actually been accomplished on the earthly plane.

The reality of a thirteenth human bodhisattva suggests that the words of Christ to His disciples about sending a new Spirit of Truth to abide on earth with them and comfort them were about a near and emergent fulfillment of the promise. To bring about this future, spiritual beings belonging to the third hierarchy would have to be especially prepared not only to revere human freedom, but to guard it against attempts to stifle it. The third hierarchy is composed of three classes of angels—angels, or guardian spirits; archangels, or group souls; and archai, or time spirits. Three such spiritual beings were active in ancient Greece. Apollo brought the beauty of Homer's epics and

Sophocles' tragedies, Philosophia the truth of Plato's Dialogues and the logic of Aristotle, and Michael the mystery centers and oracles and the spread of the glory of Greece through the journey of Alexander. Down through the Greco-Roman age and into the modern age, these guardians of freedom developed further and prepared for an advance like the one Steiner himself would later achieve. Apollo became the spirit of Catholicism, and then left the religious sphere to enter again into the realm of art and literature as the Renaissance and the spirit of Neoclassicism. Philosophia, an angel who inspired the worldviews that arose in the various philosophers, rose to a higher rank when in 1879 she took on the office of the archangel of the sun. With Steiner's efforts in writing the basic books, she came to be called Anthroposophia.[1] Michael, the sun archangel since time immemorial, also rose to a higher rank. The archangel of esoteric Christianity took on the office of Christian archai and began to bring the various religions together in harmony with the help of the Western Masters working to heal religious prejudices. By 1924, the Father Spirit granted the request of the Christ Spirit, and His power enabled three spiritual beings— Apollo, Philosophia, and Michael—to coalesce into a unity, a new Spirit of Truth, a divine bodhisattva able to abide in the earthly realm just like the Western Masters, who repeatedly experienced full incarnations on the earthly plane.

The activity of these same three spiritual beings can be observed in the three stages of the growth of the Anthroposophical movement.[2] The first stage, the seven-year cycle from 1902 to 1909—encompassing the publication of the basic books—was when philosophy became anthroposophy. The second stage, from 1909 to 1916—characterized by the production of the Mystery Dramas—involved the transformation of the Apollonian culture of the lesser mysteries of antiquity into the air trial of modern times and a more advanced form of anthroposophy. The final stage, from 1916 to 1923, featured the introduction of the social initiatives in education, medicine, and farming that aspired to help children grow to become free adults and held the promise of healing the earth as well as the human beings on it. This cycle included planting the idea of the threefold society along with the discovery of the new Spirit of Truth, a seed that will grow and mature in the next age, the age of Philadelphia, the City of Brotherly Love. Steiner's own past incarnations give further emphasis to the idea that he had worked previously with each of these three spiritual beings.[3] When he incarnated as Aristotle in ancient Greece, he worked with Philosophia and founded philosophy. Steiner's incarnation as Schionatulander placed him in the center of the Grail saga and enabled him to serve the Christian archangel, Michael, by aiding Gahmuret and sacrificing his own life to protect Parzival. Incarnating as Thomas Aquinas in medieval Paris, he became the defender of the faith, working with Catholicism (the medieval vessel for Apollo's activity) and helping to correct the intellectual form of Aristotelianism that had threatened to obscure the words of Christ held in Apollo's memory. Rudolf Steiner had served Philosophia, Michael, and Apollo in significant ways. The New Spirit of Truth, the thirteenth divine bodhisattva, thus had a personal connection with the new Master of Wisdom.

When Christ Jesus told his disciples about the new Spirit of Truth, He called him the Advocate (or Paraclete in Greek, "one called upon for aid") and said "he will guide you into all truth" (John 16:13), pointing to the activity of Philosophia/Anthroposophia within the unitary being of the thirteenth divine bodhisattva. Jesus also said that the Comforter is the Holy Spirit, who "shall bring all things to your remembrance whatsoever I have said unto you" (John 14:26). The activity of Apollo within the new Spirit of Truth is hereby indicated. Joining the activity of these two spiritual beings with the activity of Michael, the guardian of the sphere of freedom, the new Spirit of Truth wished to befriend human beings as Christ did His disciples, to recall Christ's words, to teach the truth of all things, and to baptize with the Holy Spirit. The third member of the Godhead—the Holy Spirit or the Holy Ghost—uses the third hierarchy of angels as its vehicle, or avatar, to enter the earthly realm and to bring human beings into actual contact with the godhead.

Rudolf Steiner gave a lecture in 1923 to the teachers of the first Waldorf School, one of whom was Walter Johannes Stein. His subject was Gandhi, whom he called by his honorific, Mahatma, which meant that he was naming him as a human bodhisattva. Steiner quoted from Gandhi's speech in a courtroom in India the previous year to provide an example of Michaelic speech inspired by the Spirit of Truth and as the ideal that each teacher must pursue to become a model worthy of emulation by children. When Gandhi wrote his autobiography later that decade, he fulfilled the task laid upon every initiate in the modern age who would wish to appear publicly as such. He also clarified the role that the Spirit of Truth had played in his own life in the book's very title, The Story of My Experiments with Truth. Gandhi's accomplishment in 1922 explicitly involved his relation to the Spirit of Truth bound up with his stature as a Master of Wisdom, yet Steiner also pointed to a future when even teachers may find such a power to draw upon in their everyday lessons. Forty years later, in a courtroom in South Africa, another community organizer who had been trained as a lawyer, rose at the Rivonia Trial to protest the injustice of apartheid. Nelson Mandela's speech, steeped in the new Spirit of Truth, was credited with swaying the court of world opinion so dramatically that the South African government found it in their interest to put Mandela behind bars, but not to execute

him. Mandela's autobiography, A Long Walk to Freedom—like Gandhi's—exudes the power of the Spirit
of Truth who spoke through him.

Similar events reflecting the activity of the new
Spirit of Truth may be found in 1956, in the early days
of the Civil Rights Movement in America. Dr. Martin
Luther King, Jr., gave a kind of lecture-sermon-speech
every evening at his church to inspire and comfort the
community members engaged in the Montgomery bus
boycott. It wasn't by hiding the truth, but by speaking
it, that Dr. King brought nonviolent civil disobedience
to the shores of America. Other ministers took up the
call to become Civil Rights activists. Reverend James
Lawson started a study group in 1958 to explore the
literary and religious works that Gandhi had used to
prepare the members of the Satyagraha Ashram for
their protests. Reverend Lawson even called the groups
of people who undertook such studies and engaged in
such nonviolent protests "blessed communities." John
Lewis attended Lawson's workshop and study groups.
When Dr. King and Rev. Lawson arranged a conference for college students, they each spoke about the
need for these young adults to become actively
involved. The decision to form the Student Nonviolent Coordinating Committee (SNCC) was made
shortly thereafter, and John Lewis was chosen as its
director. Lewis's autobiography, Walking With the
Wind, like those of Gandhi and Mandela, reflects the

activity of the new Spirit of Truth and the creation of the Blessed Community, a building stone of the New Jerusalem formed out of the free deeds of human beings.

The foremost event of this repetition of the Civil War in the twentieth century occurred on August 28, 1963, on the steps of the Lincoln Memorial. Dr. King spoke to the crowd gathered on the Washington Mall about the purpose of the March on Washington and its relationship to the "Declaration of Independence" and to Lincoln's "Gettysburg Address." When he stopped and turned to sit down, Mahalia Jackson whispered to him that he should tell the people about his dream. Off script and from his heart, Dr. King began to tell his audience of his vision of the future of America. His "I Have a Dream" speech is generally read aloud on the holiday set aside to honor Dr. King and the Civil Rights Movement. The memorial built on the Mall to honor Dr. King was placed between the Jefferson Memorial and the Lincoln Memorial. It was meant to bear witness to the third stage of the development of the Temple of Liberty, following the first two phases (the Founding and the Civil War proper). Human beings can bring something unique in the development of spiritual evolution that the angelic hierarchies cannot. The free deeds of men and women will prove to be the building blocks of the future, the new cosmos of love.

The Autobiography of Malcolm X rings throughout with the victory of the Spirit of Truth in the soul of

El-Hajj Malik El-Shabazz. Fard used black magic to appear as if in a physical body in Malcolm's jail cell in 1948. He also used the big lie of the mad scientist, Yacub, to implant a belief in the inequality of the races to turn the followers of the Nation of Islam into black racists. Malcolm later admitted his error and directed his efforts to building a humane organization to address the problem of white supremacy and to open lines of communication with the newly independent African nations. Building alliances with other black groups and speaking powerfully to black people were viewed by the Director of the FBI as the two most dangerous actions of those "charismatic leaders" who would seek to become the "black Messiah." By creating the Organization for African American Unity (OAAU) and visiting many African countries, El-Hajj Malik El-Shabazz became a target for J. Edgar Hoover.

Fred Hampton's death was similar to that of Malcolm X in that the FBI tried to arrange for the leaders of street gangs—this time in Chicago—to carry out their assassination plan.[4] When that plan failed, Director Hoover gave the job to a special task force of sixteen Chicago police officers assigned to State's Attorney Hanrahan's office. What is strangest about Fred Hampton's murder is that he had just turned twenty-one three months earlier. The assassinations of Malcolm X and Dr. King occurred when they were thirty-nine years old. Their activities—Malcolm X making American racism a human rights issue and taking this issue to the United Nations, and Dr. King leading a second march on Washington, the Poor People's Campaign—were deemed dangerous enough to warrant arranging their assassinations and covering them up. Fred Hampton had been chairman of the Chicago chapter of the Black Panther Party for barely one year when the State-sponsored assassination took place on December 4, 1969. He had formed the Rainbow Coalition with the Young Lords in Lincoln Park and with a white group in Uptown, and he had met with gang leaders Jeff Fort of the Blackstone Rangers and David Barkesdale of the Devil's Disciples to try to convince them to sponsor community programs like the Free Breakfast for Children Program and the Free Medical Clinic instead of acting as instruments for poisoning black neighborhoods by selling drugs. Neither the nascent Rainbow Coalition nor failed talks with gang leaders rise to the threat level of the OAAU or the Poor Peoples Campaign. The FBI must have feared the man himself and the kind of national figure he might have become to have invested so much work and energy into trying to incarcerate Fred Hampton and then attempting to cover up his assassination. The suit of the families of the slain and the survivors was won by the Hampton family and cost the state almost two million dollars. The tragedy was that so few people got to experience Fred Hampton and the Spirit of Truth that was active within him. Those who did were moved to join together and celebrate the fiftieth anniversary of his death in 2019.

The activity of the new Spirit of Truth was not limited to the social realm and the sphere of civil rights and human rights. It also entered the cultural realm and continued the development of American culture that had been founded in the nineteenth century. The essays of Emerson were able to advance further and infuse the sermons of Dr. King due to the influences of Reinholt Niebuhr and Paul Tillich, both through their theological works and their roles as personal advisers to him. In a similar way the poetry of Whitman was able to take a step further in the twentieth century through the poems of Robert Frost and e.e. cummings. The American novel, which began its development with Herman Melville and Mark Twain, gave rise to the novels of Thornton Wilder and John Hersey. The new Spirit of Truth also blazed a path for a new art form, the painting of large-scale public murals on painted on the walls of neighborhood buildings, some of which stretch for an entire block or reach five stories high to a building's top. These murals are remarkably effective in preserving communities. Like all great art, they work directly on healing and ennobling the character of those who look at them and take them in.

The new Spirit of Truth has a similar role to play in the cultural realm of the sciences. The thirteenth

Spirit of Truth must become the guide for modern materialistic science. Agriculture needs to rise from the beginnings of organic farming to that of Biodynamic farming and begin to bring cosmic forces down from the heavenly worlds and into preparations that enliven the soil and help to heal the earth. In the realm of medicine, plant remedies need to play the leading role in healing the sick. Drugs and surgery should become a last resort. Education must find a new pedagogy, one based not on Pavlov and stimulus-response psychology, but insights into the spiritual foreground of learning, growth, and development. The four temperaments in the elementary school years and the seven stages of the development of the soul, or astral body, in the high school and college years need to be understood if the ideal of educating towards freedom is to be achieved. Reverence toward the spiritual identity of the student—the ego—and a willingness to inspire each pupil as well as the whole class can enable the teacher to become a guide for the growing child— especially in the time of adolescence, that illness that everyone must live through. As Steiner indicated, the inspiration of the Spirit of Truth in the teacher prepares the growing child to accomplish a similar deed in his or her own life, transforming a job into a vocation—a calling from the spiritual world.

The task that the World Spirit places before mankind can best be characterized by saying that the earth itself needs to become a work of art. The most important reason that mankind has not been able to take up this mission yet is because it was unable to grasp the idea of a threefold society. For those who have some knowledge of the Hegelian dialectic, the difficulty can be stated as follows: The growth of capitalism from the sixteenth century onwards can be called the thesis. Its antithesis began to appear in the nineteenth century and can be called socialism. With the realization of a world economy at the beginning of the twentieth century, an opportunity arose to find the synthesis of capitalism and socialism. Unfortunately, coincident with the emergence of these two forces, private ownership of capital led to the rise of the super-wealthy, the "Robber Barons," while governmental ownership led to the entangled growth of bureaucracies. Without insight into a third method of controlling capital, a return to the stage prior to the world economy—that of national economies—was the only way forward. In his book, Threefold Society, Rudolf Steiner carefully explained that a synthesis of the two opposites does exist. Walter Johannas Stein gave lectures on it in conferences on the world economy. Steiner observed that ownership of capital should not be allowed in the economic realm because of inevitable corruption, and that its ownership by political bosses in the social realm is even more problematic. Its ownership belongs, rather, in the cultural sphere in a form much like that of a copyright. A cultural group with knowledge of the world economy could, for example, select an individual or group to run a new company or lead a business whose CEO has left. Business failures would also be the responsibility of this cultural group.[5]

Study groups on the world economy, lectures and conferences on the threefold society, and educational courses are needed to correct the faulty economic concepts that have become so widespread. People need to begin to see a path forward to an economic system that benefits all humankind. New political groups need to arise like the community-based organizing that arose in South Africa in the 1990s. Religious groups also need to contribute to the transformation of society in order that the changes in the economic and political systems may find their complement in the cultural sphere. Their efforts to help prisoners undertake their own self-development, maintain connections with their families, and begin to contribute their talents to the common good are essential. The most decisive of the changes that need to occur for the City of Brotherly Love to become a reality is the willingness of individuals to take up the sixfold path, just as in ancient India the followers of Gautama Buddha took up the eightfold path. It is none other than the Buddha, according to Steiner, who emulated the Christ with a sacrifice in lower devachan (in the region which Ptolemaic astronomy designates as the spiritual realm of Mars) in order that the will forces of present-day human beings may take up the exercises of meditation at the same time each day while also spending no more than ten or fifteen minutes a day on this task. The spiritual world needs to play an active role in the life of present-day humanity.

The victory over the forces of Sorath that is needed in the present day appears as a prophecy in *The Wonderful Wizard of Oz* by L. Frank Baum. Its symbol is the pail of water that Dorothy dumped on the Wicked Witch of the West which caused her to shrink away into nothingness. Christ Jesus called the new Spirit of Truth the Comforter when He tried to explain to the disciples what this gift from the Father God would mean to the world. Adolf Hitler was afraid of Steiner's Goetheanum for good reason, a reason that also stood behind the British attack on the Capitol Building in 1814 and its repetition by President Trump in 2021. The new Spirit of Truth can take these seeming defeats and metamorphose them into shining triumphs that can inspire all of humankind. Rudolf Steiner took the vision of the burning Goetheanum and blazed a path to the New Jerusalem, the true home of mankind in the world of Nirvana, the realm of Providence. He gave the world a meditation on the Foundation Stone of Love and opened the third gate to those who would meditate on the nineteen mantras of the First Class of the School for Spiritual Science. A similar accomplishment stands behind the seeming defeat of the forces of democracy and freedom on the steps of the Capitol Building by the Trumpian mobs of white supremacists in 2021. Not a path of meditation, but a book like the epics that founded the nations of the European peoples will lay the Wicked Witch of the West low. Whitman said of this future work of literature that it would become the "new American compact," and that he would be the spirit guide of its author. The Great American Novel will be the gift freely given by the reincarnated Dante, whose spirit guides will be the reborn Virgil and Mathilda—Whitman and Emerson.[6]

CHAPTER NINE NOTES

[1] See Rudolf Steiner, *The Riddles of Philosophy.*

[2] See Guenther Wachsmuth, *The Life and Work of Rudolf Steiner.*

[3] See Kirchner-Bockholt, *Rudolf Steiner's Mission and Ita Wegman.*

[4] See Haas, *The Assassination of Fred Hampton.*

[5] A fuller explanation of the interrelationships of all three spheres can be found in *The Threefold Social Order* by Rudolf Steiner.

[6] For more on the ideas contained in this and the previous paragraph, see the earlier work of the author: On how the spiritual world can play an active role in present day life, see *The Seven Gifts.* For in-depth analysis Baum's fairytale, see *The Prophecy of Oz.* For the author's new translation of the Foundation Stone, see *The Basic Books of Rudolf Steiner.* For more on Whitman, Emerson, and the new American compact," see *The Founding of American Culture.*

Works Referenced

BOOKS FROM WRIGHTWOOD PRESS

York, Maurice and Rick Spaulding. *Ralph Waldo Emerson: the Infinitude of the Private Man*. Wrightwood Press, 2008.

Spaulding, Rick and Maurice York. *A Sanctuary for the Rights of Mankind: The Founding Fathers and the Temple of Liberty*. Wrightwood Press, 2008.

Spaulding, Rick and Maurice York. *The Founding of American Culture*. Wrightwood Press [forthcoming].

Spaulding, Rick. *The Basic Books of Rudolf Steiner: a Compact Guide for Personal or Group Study*. Wrightwood Press, 2018.

Spaulding, Rick. *The Parzival Mystery Stream in the Twentieth Century*. Wrightwood Press, 2023.

Spaulding, Rick. *The Prophecy of Oz: the Victory of Dorothy, the Spirit of the Americas*. Wrightwood Press, 2017.

Spaulding, Rick. *The Seven Gifts*. Wrightwood Press [forthcoming].

GENERAL WORKS

Kirchner-Bockholt., Margarete and Erich Kirchner-Bockholt. *Rudolf Steiner's Mission and Ita Wegman*. Rudolf Steiner Press; Reprint edtion, 2016.

Grosse, Rudolf. *The Living Being "Anthroposophia."* Steiner Book Centre, 1986.

Haas, Jeffrey. *The Assassination of Fred Hampton: How the FBI and the Chicago Police Murdered a Black Panther*. Lawrence Hill Books, 2019.

Josephus. Translation from Louis H. Feldman, *Josephus with an English Translation*, vol. 9. Cambridge: Harvard University, 1965.

Lievegoed, Bernard. *The Battle for the Soul*. Hawthorn Press, 1996.

Gandhi, Mohandas K. *An Autobiography: The Story of My Experiments with Truth.* Translated from the original in Gujarati by Mahadev Desai. Beacon Press, 1993.

Raffel, Burton, tr. *Beowulf.* Mentor Classic, 1963.

Ravenscroft, Trevor. *The Spear of Destiny: the Occult Power Behind the Spear which pierced the side of Christ.* Samuel Weiser, Inc., 1982.

Rubin Report, March 25, 2016. "Interview with Milo Yiannopoulos." Clip of this portion of the interview at <https://www.youtube.com/watch?v=iUNRQ6aZijk>, retrieved from YouTube on February 11, 2023.

Shuré, Edouard. *The Genesis of Tragedy and the Sacred Drama of Eleusis.* Rudolf Steiner Pub. Co., 1936.

Stein, W.J. *The Ninth Century and the Holy Grail.* Temple Lodge Publishing, 2009.

Steiner, Rudolf. *The Karma of Untruthfulness. Volumes I and II.* Ruddolf Steiner Press, 2005.

Steiner, Rudolf. *The Riddles of Philosophy: Presented in an Outline of Its History.* Steiner Books; Reprint edition, 2009.

Steiner, Rudolf. *The Threefold Social Order.* SteinerBooks, 1966.

Steiner, Rudolf. *Toward a Threefold Society: Basic Issues of the Social Question.* Rudolf Steiner Publications, 2021.

Tautz, Johannes. *W.J. Stein: A Biography.* Translated by Marguerite Wood. Temple Lodge Publishing, 2015.

Wachsmuth, Guenther. *The Life and Work of Rudolf Steiner.* Garber Books, 1989.

Way, Lyndon C.S. 2021. *Trump, memes and the Alt-right: Emotive and affective criticism and praise.* Russian Journal of Linguistics 25 (3). 789–809. https://doi.org/10.22363/2687-0088- 2021-25-3-789-809

CPSIA information can be obtained
at www.ICGtesting.com
Printed in the USA
JSHW02191813O423
40324JS00001B/27